COLLECTIVE EFFICACY

IN A PLC AT WORK®

Lessons, Paradoxes, and Research
From a Turnaround District

MATT NAVO   JARED J. SAVAGE

Solution Tree | Press
a division of
Solution Tree

555 North Morton Street
Bloomington, IN 47404
800.733.6786 (toll free) / 812.336.7700
FAX: 812.336.7790

email: info@SolutionTree.com
SolutionTree.com

Visit **go.SolutionTree.com/PLCbooks** to download the free reproducibles in this book.

Printed in the United States of America

Library of Congress Cataloging-in-Publication Data

Names: Navo, Matt, author. | Savage, Jared J., author.
Title: Collective efficacy in a PLC at work : lessons, paradoxes, and
   research from a turnaround district / Matt Navo, Jared J. Savage.
Description: Bloomington, IN : Solution Tree Press, 2021. | Includes
   bibliographical references and index.
Identifiers: LCCN 2021020305 (print) | LCCN 2021020306 (ebook) | ISBN
   9781951075514 (paperback) | ISBN 9781951075521 (ebook)
Subjects: LCSH: Professional learning communities--California--Sanger. |
   School improvement programs--California--Sanger. | Educational
   change--California--Sanger. | Sanger Unified School District (Calif.)
Classification: LCC LB1731 .N348 2021 (print) | LCC LB1731 (ebook) | DDC
   371.2/07--dc23
LC record available at https://lccn.loc.gov/2021020305
LC ebook record available at https://lccn.loc.gov/2021020306

Solution Tree
Jeffrey C. Jones, CEO
Edmund M. Ackerman, President

Solution Tree Press
President and Publisher: Douglas M. Rife
Associate Publisher: Sarah Payne-Mills
Art Director: Rian Anderson
Managing Production Editor: Kendra Slayton
Copy Chief: Jessi Finn
Production Editor: Alissa Voss
Content Development Specialist: Amy Rubenstein
Proofreader: Elisabeth Abrams
Text and Cover Designer: Kelsey Hergül
Editorial Assistants: Sarah Ludwig and Elijah Oates

ACKNOWLEDGMENTS

I would like to acknowledge the leadership of Rich Smith (associate superintendent) and Marc Johnson (former superintendent) and the Sanger Unified School Board, leaders, teachers, and community for their tremendous impact on the transformation of the Sanger Unified School District. Their collective hard work, dedication, and leadership started a transformation that has continued to evolve and improve.

Finally, I would like to acknowledge my wife, Tylee Navo; my mother, Laura Orozco; my father, Mark Navo; my stepfather, Cecilio Orozco; and my children, Kennedy, Britton, and Trent Navo, for patience, guidance, belief, inspiration, and support as I took on the dream of publishing the experiences God provided me.

—Matt Navo

I would like to acknowledge Marc Johnson (former superintendent) and Matt Navo (former superintendent) for their visionary leadership; Daniel Chacon (former principal of Sanger High School) for being a mentor, coach, and field general to all of us who have served under his leadership; the Sanger Unified School Board, district and site leadership, teachers, coaches, and the Sanger community for having the courage to do *whatever it takes* for the betterment of students. Your collective commitment to *learning by doing* inspired systemwide reform and shaped the cultural values that we hold sacred.

I would like to acknowledge my father, Jack Savage, Jr., and my mother, Susan, for their unwavering belief and support; my brother, Jason "Zeus" Savage (#7)—you have always been my hero, *for I am my brother's keeper*; my son, Jacob, for making "Angel Flight" and "Happy Anywhere" our soundtrack; my grandfather, Jack Savage, Sr., for showing us what it means to live: God, family, country; and finally, all of my family and friends who continue to be part of life's journey together. Godspeed.

—Jared J. Savage

Solution Tree Press would like to thank the following reviewers:

Bre Bartels
Principal
Harbor Lights Middle School
Holland, Michigan

Katie Madigan
Principal
Glasgow Middle School
Alexandria, Virginia

Alexander Fangman
Principal
Grant's Lick Elementary School
Alexandria, Kentucky

Michael McWilliams
Principal
Savannah Elementary School
Denton, Texas

Tara Fulton
Principal
Clute Intermediate, Brazosport ISD
Clute, Texas

Jason Salhaney
Principal
Owen Intermediate School
Belleville, Michigan

Diane Kelly
Principal
Cotton Creek School
Island Lake, Illinois

Claire Springer
Assistant Principal
Savannah Elementary School
Denton, Texas

Laura Liccione
Coordinator of Academic Improvement
Maryland State Department
 of Education
Baltimore, Maryland

Visit **go.SolutionTree.com/PLCbooks** to
download the free reproducibles in this book.

TABLE OF CONTENTS

Reproducible pages are in italics.

CHAPTER 3
Building Vision to Enhance Collective Efficacy..... 53

CHAPTER 4
Building Belief and Accountability to Enhance Collective Efficacy 71

CHAPTER 5

Building Autonomy to Enhance Collective Efficacy 91

ABOUT THE AUTHORS

**Matt Navo** is the director of systems transformation at WestEd's Center for Prevention and Early Intervention. He helps districts and schools develop strategies, structures, policies, and practices that assist in closing the achievement gap for all students.

Matt specializes in aligning systems for building capacity and continuous improvement, in building collaborative cultures, and in establishing coherent and efficient systems for closing the achievement gap. He also works with the National Center for Systemic Improvement (NCSI), collaborating with state education departments and local district leaders on building improvement methodologies and continuous-improvement frameworks.

Matt has experience as a special education elementary and secondary teacher, counselor, resource teacher, junior high learning director, high school assistant principal, elementary principal, alternative education principal, director of special education, area administrator, and superintendent. He was the governor's appointee for the Advisory Commission on Special Education (ACSE) from 2014 to 2016, and the governor's appointee to the California Collaborative for Educational Excellence (CCEE) from 2016 to 2017. He is the governor's 2019 appointee for the California State Board of Education and the California Collaborative for Educational Excellence.

Matt has been a keynote speaker at numerous conferences on system improvement across the state of California and was a contributor to the ONE SYSTEM: Reforming Education to Serve All Students report of California's Statewide Task Force on Special Education in 2015. As superintendent, Matt's school district was highlighted for various achievements such as *Process and Protest—California: How Are Districts Engaging Stakeholders in LCAP Development?* and as a California District of Distinction in 2018.

Matt received a bachelor's degree in education and a master's degree in special education from California State University, Fresno. He holds a professional administrative credential, multiple-subject teaching credential, and a supplemental credential with an autism emphasis.

Jared J. Savage is the principal of Fairmont Elementary School (TK–8), in the nationally recognized, award-winning Sanger Unified School District (SUSD) in California. Savage's early experience includes playing football collegiately at Fresno State and an initial appetite to pursue a coaching career, which quickly transitioned to coaching teams of practitioners in education. Savage has worked as an educator for nineteen years as a teacher, coach, counselor, guidance learning specialist, assistant principal, and principal. His educational experiences include working from the elementary to secondary levels and building programs to support alternative education and foster care youth in Fresno County, California.

Savage specializes in synergizing teams of practitioners, with a focus on breaking the barriers of traditional mindsets and building championship school culture. Savage has used a coaching philosophy centered around building collective team efficacy to challenge and move teams within SUSD. Instituting fierce belief systems through shared leadership has been the hallmark of Savage's work to date.

Teams led by Savage have received multiple honors, including designations as a Solution Tree Model PLC School and the National Forum Schools to Watch Redesignation (received twice); and have received the California School Boards Association (CSBA) Golden Bell Award for Closing the Achievement Gap, the California Gold Ribbon, and the California PBIS Platinum Level Award for Fresno County. Savage's work has been highlighted in research studies including Marcos, Wise, Padover, Belenardo, & Loose's (2018) academic optimism study and Christina Dixon's (2019) networked improvement study. Savage has presented for various organizations, including the California National Forum Schools to Watch (in 2016 and 2019), the Supervisors of Child Welfare and Attendance (in 2017), and Project Lead the Way (PLTW, in 2017), and as a keynote speaker for Wonderful Education–Effective Implementation of Innovative Practices in California (2016).

Savage received a bachelor of arts in psychology and a master's in educational leadership from California State University, Fresno. He also holds a professional administrative credential and pupil personnel services credential.

To learn more about the work of Matt Navo or Jared J. Savage, follow @Matthew Navo and @JaredJSavage on Twitter. To book Matt Navo or Jared J. Savage for professional development, contact pd@SolutionTree.com.

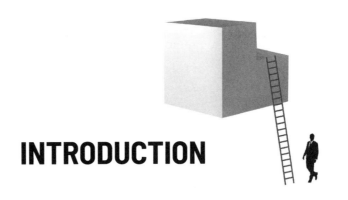

INTRODUCTION

*"Our greatest resource is
our human resource."*

—Anthony Muhammad

In all of our years of service in education, we have yet to find the "magic bullet" to improve educational outcomes. In fact, what we experienced proves that there is no magic bullet and no amount of pressure from poor test scores, humiliation, public disapproval, or bad reputation that can be used to transform a school system. Our truth, as it turns out, is that the only thing that leads to school improvement is a fundamental shift in organizational culture, directly stemming from hard work, deep collaboration, and problem solving of the people within it, powered by collective efficacy.

So, how did one of the lowest-performing school districts in the state of California become one of the state's top turnaround districts? As teachers and leaders of Sanger Unified School District, who personally experienced change from 1999 to 2021, we believe that there was one distinct reason as to why transformation occurred: building the collective efficacy fostered by professional learning communities (PLCs). Sanger's PLC journey is not without challenges, dysfunction, or conflict; in fact, it was quite the opposite. However, the rewards are plentiful for a district that anchored itself to an unshakeable belief and trust in the PLC process.

Definitions and Considerations

Collective efficacy is a powerful ingredient of the success for any school organization. Albert Bandura, the famous psychologist and originator of several social-learning theories, originally named this interesting pattern in human behavior *collective efficacy*, which he defined as "a group's shared belief in its conjoint capability to organize and execute the courses of action required to produce given levels of attainment" (Bandura, 1997, p. 477). Roger D. Goddard, Wayne K. Hoy, and

1

Anita Woolfolk Hoy (2000) define collective efficacy as a group's shared beliefs about its collective capability to promote successful student outcomes within their school.

Given these definitions of collective efficacy, and the learning experiences shared, this book uses the term *collective* to describe a convergence of team members, and *efficacy* as the belief and conviction of teams to execute the actions necessary for organizational vision attainment. It is important to note that we use *teacher efficacy* and *team efficacy* interchangeably throughout this book; neither is mutually exclusive of the other. Integral also to our definition is the belief that *team efficacy* is multi-dimensional, meaning that in order to transform our organization, we had to work at both the teacher team level and administrative team level, while at the same time building interdependence.

Although we will dig deeper into the meaning of Hattie's (2016) work in chapter 7 (page 129), we feel it necessary to reinforce the impact of collective teacher efficacy here. Rachel Eells's (2011) meta-analysis of studies related to collective efficacy and achievement in education demonstrated that the beliefs teachers hold about the ability of the school as a whole are "strongly and positively associated with student achievement across subject areas and in multiple locations" (p. 110). On the basis of Eells's research, John Hattie positioned collective efficacy at the top of the list of factors that influence student achievement (Hattie, 2016). Not only does collective teacher efficacy rank number one on Hattie's list of factors influencing student achievement, with an effect size of 1.57, collective teacher efficacy is more than double (and in some cases, triple) the effect size of other factors such as family dynamics and socioeconomic status, both with an effect size of 0.52 (Hattie, 2016).

Therefore, educators have three critical considerations when implementing programs and initiatives.

1. Recognizing and bringing awareness to the most important elements of collective teacher efficacy

2. Creating conditions necessary to foster the development of collective teacher efficacy

3. Building the competence and capacity of stakeholders around collective teacher efficacy

We believe that these considerations will help generate organizational cultures that, in turn, foster the development of collective efficacy and produce increases in student achievement.

The Necessity of Balance

Building collective efficacy requires balanced leadership. Leaders may frequently find themselves facing paradoxes when attempting to effect change in an organization.

Examples of such paradoxes, and the subsequent "balancing acts" that leaders undertake, include the following.

1. The implementation of any initiative requires leaders to provide staff members with both choice and framework.

2. Leaders must give practitioners both autonomy and feedback while carrying out the established vision and accountability models for the organization.

3. Leaders must acknowledge that ongoing learning is important for building competence and capacity, but it must be measured against results.

4. Leaders must nurture interdependence yet honor independence for individuals and teams.

5. Leaders must delicately counterbalance relationships and identity with accountability and process.

These are just some of the examples that reflect the dichotomy of leadership. It is imperative that leaders first become aware of such paradoxes (often time-opposing constructs) and then consider how to balance these within their leadership decision-making processes and practices.

Paradoxes often complicate the work of building collective efficacy of teams; however, in this book, we attempt to highlight those common paradoxes faced by leaders to alleviate confusion and uncover the realities of school leadership. The chapters in this book will reveal the genuine struggle to strike the necessary leadership balance to continue to move teams forward. We believe that if leaders can infuse the right formula of balanced leadership into the fabric of school teams and organizations, it will help foster the conditions necessary to build collective efficacy.

Sanger's Journey as a PLC

Sanger's PLC journey began in 2003, when Sanger High School was involved in a joint school improvement project with the Riverside County Office of Education. Those initial conversations led to Sanger understanding and implementing the PLC process (Johnson, 2015). Subsequently, when district leaders Marc Johnson and Rich Smith brought back the language of a PLC from a 2005 conference hosted by Rick and Becky DuFour in Palm Desert, California, the story of building collective efficacy through a PLC began to form.

From that moment, the initiative of building PLCs across Sanger's schools and district had begun. At first its site leaders were confused by the new terminology and quickly reverted to the all-too-common excuse, "We are already doing this." The assumption that grade-level meetings were the same as collaborative team meetings was shortsighted, uninformed, and based off false assumptions. Where most districts

THE LANGUAGE OF PLCs

Three big ideas drive the work of a PLC (DuFour, DuFour, Eaker, Many, & Mattos, 2016). They are:

1. A focus on learning

2. A collaborative culture and collective responsibility

3. A results orientation

A *focus on learning* requires educators to display a laser-like focus on student achievement. As DuFour et al. (2016) state, "The fundamental purpose of the school is to ensure that all students learn at high levels (grade level or higher). The focus on and commitment to the learning of each student are the very essence of a *learning* community" (p. 11). To ensure that all students learn at high levels, educators within a PLC must work *collaboratively* and assume *collective responsibility* for each student's success. As a result, collaborative teacher teams with mutual accountability are essential to the structure of PLCs. Finally, a *results orientation* means educators in a PLC place emphasis on student outcomes. They use evidence of learning to inform and improve their teaching practice and create enrichment or intervention opportunities for students in their care.

The four critical questions of the PLC process are:

1. What knowledge, skills, and dispositions should every student acquire as a result of this unit, this course, or this grade level?

2. How will we know when each student has acquired the essential knowledge and skills?

3. How will we respond when some students do not learn?

4. How will we extend the learning for students who are already proficient?

Rather than assuming a deficit-based approach to student outcomes—for example, focusing on "What is wrong with this particular student or group of students?"—collaborative teacher teams can demonstrate their commitment to the three big ideas of PLCs by collectively discussing these critical questions.

would have adopted PLC system change first, Sanger's approach was different. Leaders specifically focused on enhancing professional relationships and communication that ultimately led to increased trust and collaboration. The building blocks set the stage for a full adoption of the PLC process.

There was a realization that adding a new initiative, PLCs, to the goals of the district was not the best first step if leadership was to address negative emotions and convictions about the history of numerous organizational change initiatives. Leaders came to realize that any positive intentions of PLCs, no matter how valuable, would be seen as "here we go again," and resistance would be part of every team's mental makeup regardless of the benefits.

With time, and dedication to the implementation of the PLC process, the district that had once been ranked as California's ninety-eighth-worst school district in 2004 and one of only seven school districts that were subject to Program Improvement (PI) requirements under federal law became one of the state's most successful school districts (Smith, 2015). Seven years later, Sanger had moved all of its schools out of PI status, and four schools went on to achieve the designation of State Distinguished Schools (David & Talbert, 2013). The district had done this through an interconnected, continuous journey of building schoolwide and districtwide PLCs and, as a result, discovering the importance of how to build collective team efficacy.

Sanger learned that building PLCs and collective team efficacy is an ongoing challenge, one that requires cultivation, innovation, and rejuvenation year after year. What its leadership discovered set Sanger on a path toward understanding the following core principles that changed their ability to work collectively together.

- **Principle 1:** PLCs and team efficacy require continuous improvement processes, always beginning and never ending.

- **Principle 2:** PLCs and team efficacy are about both student *and* adult learning.

- **Principle 3:** PLCs and team efficacy are built through collective commitments, beliefs, willingness, and the capability to trust each other and enhance professional relationships.

Stage 1 of Sanger's transformation connected to principle 1: PLCs and team efficacy have to be a continuous improvement process, always beginning and never ending. This stage was a challenge for leaders. Prior to the PLC process being a priority initiative, other initiatives were more about check-the-box-style compliant behavior. Leaders quickly focused on compliance, rarely paying attention to the impact of the compliance (be it negative or positive). This irritated many of the teachers and was the reason for many failed, yet well-intended, initiatives. With PLC implementation, as educators focused on getting their tasks done, they also had to focus on building a continuous improvement mindset where the journey to "good enough" never ends. Rather, it is about getting better at getting better.

That's where Sanger truly began understanding the work of PLCs and came to realize that the organization was in this for the long haul. This was, as Simon Sinek in his book *The Infinite Game* (2019) would term it, a "just cause." PLCs became the "just cause" of what Sanger desired to become. Leadership set a course to become an organization that worked together interdependently and collaboratively to improve student results. Sanger's leaders started by diving into *Learning by Doing* (DuFour, DuFour, Eaker, & Many, 2006), discussing the meaning and setting the stage for idea sharing, potential implementation challenges, and goal setting. Stage 1 was all about building teacher and leader capacity and capability to understand, know, and do the work of PLCs.

Stage 2 was connected to principle 2: PLCs and team efficacy are about both student *and* adult learning. Leaders had to embrace learning as adults. Learning how to behave and become a collaborative team is not the same as *saying* you are one, and this was difficult for leaders to wrap their heads around. As much as teams wanted to make PLCs about student learning, Sanger found that it is equally essential to think about adult learning within a PLC. Learning how to be a professional learning community is different than just being professional. Professional, honest relationships were key to behaving like a PLC and building the collective belief that the work could be done.

Stage 3 was connected to principle 3: PLC and team efficacy is built through collective commitments, beliefs, willingness, and the capability to trust each other and enhance our professional relationships. Sanger's leaders had to accept that they could not do this work alone. They needed a guiding coalition of professionals at the school site who would undoubtedly become the PLC "culture keepers" of the school and district efforts. They needed believers (or *early adopters* as school culture expert Anthony Muhammad refers to them)—people who have an early desire to move away from the negative noise to a more positive tune. As more and more staff members came to discover the impact of the change, they developed a belief in each other that eventually led to improved collective team efficacy and student outcomes.

Ultimately, Sanger's journey as a PLC resulted in noticeably improved collective efficacy that directly and positively impacted the lives of not just the students in the district but also its staff, leaders, and wider community.

About the Book

This book highlights, for K–12 teachers, school teams, team coaches, administrators, and practitioners, the efforts of the Sanger Unified School District, and the lessons we learned as the organization sought to transform our school site teams, schools, and district—an effort that eventually led to a district turnaround. As members and leaders of the Sanger Unified team for over a decade, we will speak to the paradoxes, research, and lessons that impacted our experiences and tenure. New and veteran practitioners alike will gain valuable insight into the importance of collective efficacy at all levels of the school organization in three critical areas: (1) balanced leadership, (2) how to build and empower teams, and (3) collective learning with a systematic response.

The first six chapters focus on building six different aspects to enhance collective efficacy. Chapter 1 discusses changing organizational *culture*, exploring efforts to change a toxic culture of dysfunction into one of intentionality and reflection by utilizing Margaret J. Wheatley's (1992) concept of *below the green line* (BTGL). Chapter 2 stresses the importance for teams to discover their *purpose*—the connection to something greater than themselves. Leaders that help teams find the "right *why*" speak to the heart of human beings and develop hope around a compelling message. In chapter 3, we examine the importance of unleashing the power of a meaningful *vision* that incorporates and involves all stakeholders in the crafting of the vision through collaboration. Chapter 4 then presents our case that *belief and accountability* are essential components in building collective team efficacy. When leaders can inspire through non-negotiable beliefs and convictions, teams cultivate an ability to take on challenging situations. In chapter 5, we discuss the process for using integrity as the reward for *autonomy* to build the collective commitments of teacher teams. We explore why merely having norms may not be enough for some teams, and how using autonomy to build and reinforce behaviors is crucial for building collective efficacy. Then, in chapter 6, we finalize our story by putting the focus on *collaboration* as the foundation for building collective team efficacy.

Chapter 7 then combines all these lessons together and introduces our Theory of Action, a framework of understanding for how teams assess and build collective team efficacy and how teams can identify the types of experiences they need to foster and enhance collective team efficacy. In the epilogue, we tie everything together so teams can internalize the clear and compelling case for prioritizing collective efficacy. Lastly, to assist teams in measuring and improving collective efficacy, we share tools, resources, and processes at the end of each chapter as well as in the appendix.

The first six chapters include the following sections.

- **The Challenge:** This opening section provides a description of the organizational experience and sets the context for the chapter.

- **The Change:** This section describes the change event (or events) that Sanger's leadership instituted to address the identified challenge.

- **Leadership Paradoxes:** This section defines the specific paradoxes that challenged team collective efficacy during a specific time period and helps leaders and teachers see the balance required to successfully build collective efficacy.

- **Leadership Research:** This section reflects on the research that helps define the paradoxes discovered previously.

- **Reflection Questions:** This section provides the reader an opportunity to reflect on what has been shared thus far and gives them thoughts to consider as they work to improve collective team efficacy in their own districts.

- **Leadership Lessons:** In this section, we present our learnings from the challenge we experienced as we sought to build collective team efficacy.

- **Practitioner Perspectives:** These insights and experiences from various practitioners within Sanger Unified School District bring to life the lessons individual teachers learned during that specific time in the turnaround journey.

- **Conclusion:** This section allows us to consolidate the learning of the chapter into one succinct lesson that gives practitioners considerations for building collective team efficacy in their own schools.

- **Next Steps:** Each chapter includes a 1–5–10 rating tool to assist teams in evaluating their current reality against a standard of essential elements that help build collective team efficacy. Self-assessment must occur first, followed by teams collectively assessing the sum of their findings. This will lead to a quick organizational acknowledgment and provide potential changes that are connected to the overarching themes for leadership. The 1–5–10 tools pave the way for increased awareness and further alignment in key areas most valued by the organization.

Our Hope

The book highlights some of the most important experiential lessons for us as both leaders and practitioners. As you explore the following chapters, please consider our hope for this book: that you, as educators, consider creating the conditions necessary to foster collective team efficacy that will directly and positively impact the lives of children. It is important to underscore the profound and lasting impact that collective efficacy can have on school organizations. Universal educational constructs such as leadership, vision, culture, and collaboration are all undeniably influenced by collective efficacy, for better or for worse. Therefore, if leaders can learn and create the conditions necessary to foster high levels of collective team efficacy, school organizations are more likely to experience the changes necessary to attain higher levels of student achievement.

Finally, we ask that you reflect; find parallels to your own story; and apply the paradoxes, research, and lessons we learned at Sanger Unified to the schools and organizations you serve. We truly hope that by reading this book, you may learn vicariously through our experience, hardships, and insights that will help to build collective efficacy for your organization.

CHAPTER 1

BUILDING CULTURE TO ENHANCE COLLECTIVE EFFICACY

"The culture in which we live, and with which we identify, powerfully shapes just about every aspect of our being."

—Angela Duckworth

In 2018, Jenni Donohoo, John Hattie, and Rachel Eells wrote, "Since collective efficacy influences how educators feel, think, motivate themselves, and behave, it is a major contributor to the tenor of a school's culture" (p. 41). There is a vast amount of research on collective efficacy and its origins, showing that collective efficacy is born in beliefs. This nexus of perceptions, convictions, and thoughts that people hold—beliefs they may be aware or unaware they hold—has a powerful impact on effort expenditure, motivation, and resiliency attributes. Donohoo et al. (2018) address the role of evidence and its impact on building collective team efficacy, stating, "Evidence of collective impact, in turn, reinforces proactive collective behaviors, feelings, thoughts, and motivations" (p. 42). Psychologist Albert Bandura (1997) reinforces this notion of collective impact having positive consequences, referring to it as *reciprocal causality* and noting that collective efficacy is "a social resource that doesn't get depleted by its use, it gets renewed" (p. 42).

This chapter introduces the transformation of the Sanger Unified School District, highlighting both the dysfunction of the city and the school district. It brings to light some changes that helped jump-start a districtwide cultural transformation in a district that was plagued by a lack of collaboration, trust, and mutual accountability. While the transformation of the district is still a work in progress, major changes occurred between 1999 and 2007, during which the school board leadership, district leadership, site leadership, and team leadership groups were all challenged to make a choice to either change for the better or remain in an ongoing state of stress and confrontation. The three core principles highlighted in the introduction (page 5) helped Sanger shape mindsets to begin and engage district stakeholders in the PLC process. Sanger had to shift thinking about PLC development and separate it from the "this too shall pass" mentality that had plagued the district for many years.

As leaders moved, unknowingly at the time, through the three stages and principles, they began to discover the benefits of the PLC process. As they pulled the PLC lever collectively, a gate opened, and collective belief began to flow through. This greater awareness and deeper understanding led to the realization that collective team efficacy is a powerful antecedent to positive school culture and student outcomes.

The Challenge: "The Home of 400 Unhappy Teachers"

In March of 1999, if you drove thirteen miles east of California Highway 41, down a seven-mile stretch of Jensen Avenue in Fresno County, you would eventually pass the small, rural town of Sanger. The Sanger Unified School District in 1999 comprised approximately 9,000 students in a town of around 18,700 residents. Orange orchards and vineyards surrounded the small, rural farming community. The history of the small town was very apparent to a new visitor. Undeveloped and untouched by the changes of modern times, the hub of the town on Fridays was the local Kmart, its parking lot loaded with cars and families making their runs for supplies. However, most striking on the drive into town was the beauty of the Sierra Nevada mountains atop the eastern skyline.

The reputation of Sanger Unified, at that time, was less than stellar. The district was known for having a high propensity for gang violence in its schools, low student achievement results, public school board political drama, and, as a result, high teacher and administrative turnover. This backdrop may sound eerily similar to other rural small-town school districts, if not for the following small, but important, detail.

At the end of the main road, two significant indicators of the town's identity would come into view. Just before the giant K-Mart appeared the city's seal: a large round plaque that read, "Welcome to Sanger, home of the nation's Christmas tree city!" Sanger was identified as the nation's Christmas tree city because it was the last major town on the road to the Kings Canyon and Sequoia National Park, where General Grant, an awe-inspiring giant sequoia tree that many visitors come to admire over the years, is located. According to the Sanger Chamber of Commerce, the U.S. Post Office anointed the City of Sanger as the nation's Christmas tree city on October 1, 1949 (Sanger District Chamber of Commerce, n.d.), and the citizens of this town took great pride in its advertising. However, what was above that sign would take viewers from a place of great pride to one of confusion and disappointment.

There, above the city's prized identity, was a large green sign, about the size of those seen while driving on the freeway, that said, "Welcome to Sanger: Home of 400 Unhappy Teachers!" For new teachers entering the district for the first time, reading that sign would be heartbreaking at worst and demoralizing at best. For existing teachers, the sign was a cry for help. Questions circulated within the district: who put the sign up? And what were they hoping to accomplish? Regardless of the theories, the famous sign begged two questions: (1) how bad could the school district culture be? and (2) what does it say about a community that tolerates it? Not only did the sign bury the culture of the school district under a shroud of dysfunction, it demoralized the city and polarized the city against the school district.

The climate of the community and school district at the time of the sign involved a vocal union leadership and an equally vocal disgruntled community. Employees of the district seemed to always be engaged in discussions regarding potential strikes, although by 1999, it was clear that the lack of positive culture of the district, highlighted in negotiations between the district and the Sanger Unified Teachers Association (SUTA) and California School Employees Association (CSEA), had put the community at odds and forced them to take sides. Most of the community had grown tired of what they considered to be a lack of competence and confidence in the board and district leaders. There were those in the community that believed hardline leadership involving telling the teachers what they have to do was the answer, and others who felt leadership needed to go.

The internal dysfunction that embattled the school board for years also plagued the City Council of Sanger. The City Council wanted to run the district, and the school district wanted to run the city. For its part, the community wanted change, and so members of the public frequently packed both public meeting locations. School board meetings were held in the eight-hundred-seat capacity high school auditorium to accommodate the large mass of people who disagreed with the decisions and direction of the school district. Board members were often accused of outlandish behavior, district administrators were consistently questioned on conduct and decision making, and the community wasn't exactly viewed as the epicenter for potential teachers or future leaders who sought to build a career or raise a family.

Essentially the district had failed to build clarity, focus, engagement, and commitment to any initiative and, as a result, had failed to build a positive culture. In the end, the only things holding the community and district together were the traditions, pride, and rituals that occurred whenever Sanger student athletes took to the field. It was not uncommon to hear someone say, "A good football season can make a lot of problems seemingly disappear."

With every failed initiative came a new idea. With every new idea came confusing guidance and implementation. Principals and teachers figured out how the culture of the district worked—if you could hunker down, work in isolation, and not draw attention to yourself, then you might survive. And that became the cultural mentality of the district: isolation and survival.

During the 1999–2000 school year, a new Sanger superintendent, one with new ideas and who was considered by many to be a forward thinker, couldn't get initiatives off the ground because of the inability to build a sense of team relationship and efficacy. Even though the ideas had merit and promise, there was no culture that could move them. This meant the leadership methods needed to push the new initiatives forward were more divisive than collective, more directive than collaborative. This fostered and increased district divisiveness. Nowhere was this more visible than at the district's lone high school.

There always comes a moment of epiphany for leaders of teams, during which the realization of just how bad things are becomes suffocating, and panic can set in. This moment, which underscores the deep level of dysfunction Sanger was experiencing, occurred in early 2000, when a fantastic, energetic high school English teacher walked into the assistant principal's office on Friday afternoon. As the teacher stepped into the office, it was obvious to the young administrator that something was seriously wrong. When the assistant principal asked what the matter was, the teacher replied, "I quit! They slashed my tires!"

Unfortunately, at that particular time this wasn't an uncommon statement by teachers. Sanger had a large gang presence, and the community and district were often plagued by gang violence and gang activity, which occasionally included the slashing of tires. The difference in this instance was that the teacher believed the slashing had not been propagated by students but rather by his *fellow teachers*, out of frustration that he would not consider striking with them. (It was later discovered that this teacher really had no proof to determine if it was teachers, other staff, or students who had slashed his tires. However, the culture of the district was so grim that he was led to believe the other teachers would indeed be capable of such an act.)

Hearing that statement would be enough to sit any administrator back in their chair. For this assistant principal of Sanger High, it was an epiphany—the moment the district hit complete rock bottom. There was no belief either from the teacher or the assistant principal that any good could come out of such a situation. Teachers had no allegiance to anything more than protecting themselves and their students—and that sometimes meant fighting, both overtly and covertly. Collective team efficacy had been built around fighting the system that had failed them so many times. The discovery for this assistant principal, who would later become superintendent of Sanger USD, was that Sanger lacked collective team efficacy and a culture of belief and trust in each other, and was instead focused on fighting poor student achievement results instead of fighting to improve bad culture. It was a discovery that began to play out in almost every grade- and content-level team he worked with. Where there was conflict within a team, there existed a lack of belief and trust amongst and within the team.

Over the course of the next two years (1999–2001), the district continued to be embroiled in heated battles due to ongoing adversarial relationships between leadership, teachers, and the community. Community members were enraged about potential school strikes, teachers were furious about the lack of support, and leadership was engulfed in exhausting district turmoil. A dejected organizational culture of low commitment and a lack of coherence led to poor confidence and significant distrust. All of the disarray led to a sad truth: the students paid the biggest price for a failed culture.

The Change

By the end of 2002, a new culture was on the horizon, and the days of students being secondary priorities were about to start coming to an end. As the community dysfunction raged on, several board members were up for reelection. With this opportunity, two new individuals were being more vocal about proclaiming different philosophies and values. Board members Pete Filippi and Jim Karle had declared that transparency and trust of the school board would be top priorities. Their platforms had moved away from the idea that the board should be micromanaging the district; instead they believed it should prioritize a culture of learning for students first, not political dogma or ideology. It was a new philosophy, a firm approach, and one that Sanger desperately needed. The community embraced the opportunity for change, and with the opportunity of change, the board took bold steps to make a huge cultural shift from what would have been a single new superintendent model to a shared leadership model. Ultimately, for a period of time, the board actually dissolved the role of superintendent and instead required the human resources, curriculum and instruction, and business departments to share decision-making roles. In this model, new ideas and initiatives could not be started without consensus from the three assistant superintendents. It was a model that began to build a collaborative structure without knowing it. This was the first big step toward building collaboration and collective team efficacy. However, this time the biggest difference was the change that started with leadership at the top.

With this new collaboration structure came an enhanced communication effort that evolved into a new district-level composition made up of shared leadership and decision making. The model led to an eventual appointment of a new superintendent in Marc Johnson, a leader who believed in collaboration and problem solving. It also led to a perfect match between the superintendent and the PLC model. When Marc and former assistant superintendent Rich Smith heard the PLC story from Rick and Becky DuFour in 2005, the model resonated with them, and they felt like they had a way of prioritizing student learning and a way to improve the district.

However, Sanger's leaders were perplexed by the challenge of creating the conditions necessary to foster a positive, caring, intentional organizational culture that put students first. There were no systems or structures in place to reinforce the hope of building a PLC culture anchored to collective team efficacy, and, as Rich Smith and Marc Johnson would say, "Hope is not a strategy" (R. Smith & M. Johnson, personal communication, February 1, 2003). To change Sanger's current reality to achieve something greater, its leaders would need to rethink the inner workings of the entire organization, including the subtle but powerful nuances of culture of which leaders are typically unaware. The new vision for culture would demand the confrontation of ineffective practices through self-reflection, the development of improved instructional and collaborative strategies, and the collective alignment of beliefs and behaviors—not simply hope.

Under Marc Johnson's leadership, Sanger's leaders aimed to improve the district by taking the following steps (Johnson, 2015).

1. Develop a shared mission, vision, values, and goals.

2. Build a collaborative culture focused on student learning.

3. Build collective understanding of what works and what doesn't.

4. Establish continuous improvement through a learning by doing approach.

5. Be results oriented.

This approach began to help Sanger move the needle on improving team collective efficacy. To change culture you must start at the top, and by anchoring their change effort to the PLC process, Sanger unknowingly (and, in many cases, unintentionally) built team efficacy—the key ingredient, they discovered, in improving team and organization culture.

PRACTITIONER PERSPECTIVE

"As assistant superintendent in 1999, and later superintendent in 2003, I found that the most difficult issue, as an outsider looking in, was the lack of trust between management and practitioner. No matter what I said, we rarely found common ground. Working on our culture forced us all to reconsider how we did the work and why we did the work. We may not have convinced everyone, but we cultivated a collaborative culture and convinced enough people that we improved all of our schools, dramatically improved student learning outcomes, and developed high-functioning collaborative teams at all sites."

—**Marc Johnson**
*Assistant Superintendent 1999–2002, Superintendent 2003–2013,
National Superintendent of the Year 2011*

The new vision of culture was that the system would be deeply rooted in professional relationships and the power of interdependence. The leadership of the district also wanted to foster a positive, caring, intentional organizational culture that put students first. Why was this new vision the answer to the many cultural problems Sanger was facing? Because the history of the district, and behaviors of the past, had put the district on a hamster wheel of frustration, defeat, and nonperformance, the individuals within the district had been so concerned about protecting themselves and the other adults that they had systematically forgotten about the students. The aim was to get off the hamster wheel by changing and charging forward with principles that shift the way people talk about the work.

Between 2003 and 2018, Sanger adopted some very simple yet powerful principles that began to shift the culture.

- Hope is not a strategy.
- Don't blame the kids.
- It's all about student learning.
- Believe all kids can and must learn.

These principles guided the transformation of a culture that leaders embraced and that, slowly but surely, other stakeholders began to adopt. The principles were imprinted on the minds of leaders, teachers, and community members. They were recited, stated, and exclaimed at every meeting, every gathering, and every training as guardrails for language that represented Sanger's new belief system.

As the district adopted a new vernacular, the evolution took on another mindset shift, and the work of Margaret Wheatley (1992) came to the forefront. The district contracted with Steve Zuieback, president and owner of management consulting firm Synectics, to help identify some of the deeply rooted issues Sanger's teachers and administrators were having difficulty moving beyond. Steve worked Sanger's educators through conversations that involved tears, anger, frustration, and doubt. Most importantly, he exposed Sanger's leaders to Margaret Wheatley's Six-Circle Model (1992), which we termed *below the green line* (described in more detail in "Visible vs. Invisible," page 19). The model, originally developed by Margaret Wheatley and later modified by Tim Dalmau and Richard Knowles, was a game-changer for Sanger!

Sanger's leaders adopted the *below the green line* concept in its entirety. Teachers began to understand the mental model of what they had been trying to share in the display of "the sign" years before. Working *below the green line* became an everyday mantra. And the Six-Circle Model helped leaders and teachers develop a mental model for the dysfunction that was occurring.

Leaders pushed the honest conversation mantra to the front of PLCs, stating, "If we are going to get better at getting better, then we have to be willing to be honest about our work. And it starts by looking at student results—data." The PLC process, for the first time, began to shift in two ways.

1. Sanger teams were focused on honest, professional conversations.
2. Sanger teams were beginning to use student data to guide their conversations.

These may seem like minor changes, but for Sanger it was the impetus for a new paradigm shift in building a culture of collective team efficacy within the PLC process. Most importantly, from this work Sanger teams started to believe!

By 2005, site leaders, having watched the new collaborative leadership model, began to see the walk matching the talk. This was the key that opened the door to a new vision of building a PLC culture. As the work of PLCs scaled across the district, the staff remained cautiously optimistic about this new initiative being here to stay. All Sanger needed was a little balance between consistency and change—they had to change, but also needed to balance the speed, volume, and feelings associated with new initiatives that could potentially send stakeholders into a "here we go again" state. What Sanger needed was focus, clarity, engagement, and commitment to PLCs fostered by a vision for culture change. The attention to consistency and change would bring a balance that would help to foster a new cultural reality.

As site leaders continued to buy in, new ideas, different perspectives, and fresh sets of eyes for reimagining the possibilities for Sanger schools came to life. Though most leaders embraced the value of PLCs, some leaders were unfortunately unable to visualize the benefits of a cultural change. Several had built their profession on the old, siloed, and fragmented system. They preserved themselves by not having to improve, and instead simply existing. With the new focus on collaboration as a result of the PLC process, leaders were forced to use different leadership skills. They had to become more skilled at having focused goals, clarity on how to get there, and engagement and commitment of all staff to the PLC process. In the end, some had to move on, and this created new opportunities for new leadership. New leaders brought with them no prior knowledge of the past and were simply focused on building a culture that inspired them to lead. Sanger needed leaders who could breathe belief and passion into teams, and new leaders brought that air to breathe. Sanger needed skilled collaborators and believers, and new leaders were brought in who had the skill.

Leaders, teachers, and the community had no choice but to think outside the box for solutions. This opportunity kick-started a fundamental new redesign of the district culture that ultimately impacted Sanger's leadership, school, and site teams. The redesign looked very different, and it started at the top. The district's leadership model of shared decision making worked for site leaders, who shared leadership of the PLC process with leads and department heads. This led to stakeholders who had more involvement and were able to make more contributions. Teachers' capacity and capability to participate and lead PLCs were built and shared. Ultimately, the redesign enhanced clarity, focus, engagement, and commitment to the PLC process. The impact was a new culture, one that staff were clearly able to see led to a greater desire and belief that the culture could change. And with that belief came a belief in teams' abilities and efficacy.

Leadership Paradoxes

The momentum for a cultural shift anchored in PLCs led to a unique discovery: leadership was awash with paradoxes. Paradoxes are contradictions, tensions in the work. For Sanger it was a balance of pros and cons to the approach to learning discoveries. Sanger's teachers and leaders had a history of fully engulfing themselves in silos and of every man and woman looking out only for him- or herself. Now they were being asked to behave and believe differently. Steve Zuieback's (2012) work, along with Wheatley's (1992) research, provided the jolt and collective understanding of what had been wrong all those past years. This new revelation of Sanger's past led to discoveries of the future paradoxes they would encounter.

The specific leadership paradoxes Sanger's leadership encountered when building culture to enhance collective efficacy were:

- Systems vs. people
- Confidence vs. humility
- Consistency vs. change
- Confrontation vs. support
- Visible vs. invisible

Systems vs. People

Sanger's first leadership challenge as an organization was attempting to create a different approach that balanced new systematic structures with ongoing professional development. To use this approach, the organization needed to refocus and present a new rationale to staff members and the community to justify the change—meaning, we needed to reinvent the *why* of the organization.

Our initial priority and reason for *systems* development was to identify ineffective practices within the organization and across teams. To do this, we first needed to investigate what effective practices looked and sounded like. We operationalized this investigation in the form of a leadership challenge. Leaders created a series of professional development opportunities for leaders that focused on providing valid examples of high-quality, efficient systems for businesses or school organizations. Leadership tapped into themes such as those proposed by Peter Drucker (1992), quoted in Schmoker (2016) as saying, "efficiency is doing the things right; effectiveness is doing the right things" (p. 31).

As a district, the challenge was not only to fully understand how to become, as Drucker (1992) states, both efficient and effective, but also to somehow use the connectedness (namely, the *people*) to drive cultural change. Recall that the new vision of organizational culture was that the system would be deeply rooted in relationships and the power of interdependence. Leaders were challenged, as they created their examples of high-quality efficient systems, to be consistently mindful of people, including their perceptions, feelings, and anxieties, while at the same time recognizing that the systems served as valuable tools to provide evidence of success (or lack thereof). Staff development needed to become just as important as system development.

Confidence vs. Humility

Any attempt to change an organization's culture and identity requires both confidence and humility. At Sanger, we found the leadership challenge required leaders to convey high levels of *confidence*, because there was so much historical context embedded within the district's current dysfunctional identity that even mentioning a change of any kind was met with sarcasm and flippant reactions. Leaders needed to display confidence to stand their ground and "stick to the why" in the face of inevitable opposition from staff members and the community alike. The pride and traditions of the Sanger community were deeply rooted; therefore, leaders walked a fine line between confidently creating a case for change and offending the community stakeholders. *Humility*, however, was the equalizer to confidence. The organization discovered in board meetings that the community viewed leaders who conducted themselves with a sense of humility as being both respectable and trustworthy. As district leaders demonstrated a balance between confidence and the humility of acknowledging the organization's errors, a shift occurred. The board meeting crowds began to shrink, the topics became less hostile, the district communication was more collaborative, and the communication was no longer about top-down direction but rather new change ideas from the bottom up. The paradox between confidence and humility was a leadership trait Sanger needed to continue to grow. As a result, we challenged our leaders with maintaining humility, empathy, and regard for others while at the same time communicating confidence in all circumstances.

Consistency vs. Change

Sanger's leaders needed to delicately balance *consistency* while justifying the need for *change*. Leaders had to assess the district processes, procedures, structures, and programs that were currently in place. This process required that leaders partake in substantial fact-finding, investigating various data sets as well as both formal and informal surveys to gather evidence and opinions. The organization consistently had to make difficult collective decisions to either maintain consistency with current systems or remove them from the bank of resources and initiatives the district had stockpiled. Leaders needed to balance the advantages of overhauling systems with the desire from many staff members to keep existing systems from changing. Change always seemed to be something many teachers and administrators felt Sanger needed to do—until it involved changes to their behaviors, their practices, or their beliefs. It might have been easier to not fight that resistance and remain anchored instead to those early adopters who had a desire to change. However, for meaningful change to occur, leaders realized they needed to stay consistent to the changes that were associated with the new vision of a new culture while simultaneously maintaining the fortitude to take on tough conversations, build commitment to a new beginning, avoid being negotiated out of change, and show willingness to engage in positive debate regarding the change efforts of the district. Maintaining consistency with what was working while at the same time always inviting innovation and changes were no small balancing act, but were greatly needed to build collective efficacy.

Confrontation vs. Support

In addition to attempting to change organizational culture, a stark, somewhat overwhelming reality presented itself. Leaders were faced with the prospect of having to directly *confront* the behaviors of individuals and teams that did not align with or reflect the new vision for their organizational culture. To do this, the district would need to challenge historical norms, setting a precedent for new behaviors, expectations, and reciprocal accountability. In addition, leaders had to muster up the willpower to take an unfiltered, honest assessment of the organization's broken identity, inaccurate information, and dysfunctional relationships. It is important to note that confrontation, although uncomfortable for most, should not be interpreted as heated exchanges of screaming and yelling. However, leaders needed to directly and unapologetically challenge underlying beliefs and perceptions of the organization if they were ever going to have a chance of building a new culture with collective efficacy at its core.

Support, on the other hand, needed to be authentic, collaborative, and cooperative. Support included opportunities for professional growth, making resources readily available, and dialoguing with teams about their ideas and solutions. The challenge for leaders was identifying the appropriate time and strategy to respectfully engage individuals and teams while providing the right levels of support or confrontation needed to improve team efficacy.

Visible vs. Invisible

The school board and district administration had spent year after year tweaking the obvious, *visible* components of strategy, structure, and operation of the organization, only to run into failure after failure. Despite their best efforts, including showcasing the results of change efforts they had implemented, the district's modified strategic plans, compliance forms, board policies, and organization charts did not create any form of fundamental change. Instead, there was an abundance of head-scratching and individuals asking, "Why isn't this working?"

Sanger's failures weren't a result of leaders not clearly seeing what needed to be done to improve strategy, structure, and operations. Rather, it was more that leadership had failed to understand that these changes, though they may be more visible, only represented the surface-level functions of the entire district system. Below the surface was an *invisible* underbelly to the organization that would prove unpleasant and contentious. The technical changes often pursued by leadership were mostly visible and easily accessible to the public and organizational eye. However, it was the desperate need for unabated attention and responsiveness to the organization relationships, identity, and communication that necessitated the transformative cultural change.

Leadership Research

The following research helps to complement and build on the paradoxes Sanger's leadership discovered in the challenge. The paradox of discoveries leads us to consider research that either complements or challenges what we learned.

We reviewed research for each of the paradoxes described in the previous section:

- Systems vs. people
- Confidence vs. humility
- Consistency vs. change
- Confrontation vs. support
- Visible vs. invisible

Systems vs. People

There is no question that successful school organizations and teams require high-quality systems, including structures, strategies, and processes. Without high-quality systems, there is no feasible way to evaluate the implementation and progress of programs or initiatives. Teams would be left with subjective opinions, not objective evidence, regarding successes or failures. According to Bloomberg and Pitchford (2017) in *Leading Impact Teams: Building a Culture of Efficacy,* "high-performance teams need architecture: they need a design to be productive and infrastructure to do the work. The bricks and mortar are the organizational structures and processes required to do business" (p. 27). Bloomberg and Pitchford (2017) further stress the importance of systems, contending that teams need protocols and rules of engagement to be both "efficient and effective" (p. 30). In contrast, most leaders would almost certainly claim that the people within the organization—and the relational value of leaders and teams—are even more important than its systems. Bloomberg and Pitchford (2017) fortify their claim stating, "Relational trust is the connective tissue of working relationships and is central to building effective learning communities" (p. 29). Additionally, Daniel Goleman (2013) finds that relationship skills account for nearly three times as much impact on organizational performance as analytical skills do. Therefore, in order for leaders to build collective efficacy of teams, they must ensure that their organizational efforts, resources, and expenditures maintain a balance between the desire to improve systems and the need to improve relationships with teams.

Confidence vs. Humility

School leaders must balance confidence and humility. Psychologist Albert Bandura (1977) studied the relationship between confidence levels and success. Bandura found that increased self- and team confidence led to higher success and performance rates for individuals and teams. Leader confidence is often demanded by the sheer nature of leadership positions and authority. However, it must be countered with authenticity and humility.

In his book *Primary Greatness*, author Stephen R. Covey (2015) asserts, "Humility is the mother of all virtues" (p. 18). He further states, "Humility helps us center our lives on principles, the need for ongoing character development, and helps us be considerate of others" (Covey, 2015, p. 18). Leaders of school organizations must maintain humility and regard for others even when circumstances require confidence. School leaders of teams must be willing to admit their shortcomings, challenges, and anxieties to engage the team and help team members share their own vulnerabilities.

Consistency vs. Change

Consistency is a powerful construct that school leaders need to consider when leading teams or organizations. In *Motion Leadership: The Skinny on Becoming Change Savvy*, Michael Fullan (2010) writes, "The more committed you are to relentless consistency, the more naturally you seek improvements. Today's relentless consistency is tomorrow's innovation, and tomorrow's innovation is the next day's relentless consistency" (p. 56). However, leaders must consider the other side of "relentless consistency"—change. There are large amounts of research related to change; the following studies are just a few examples that illustrate the dimensions of change.

A quote attributed to Charles Darwin (1809–1882) brings the concept of change into clear focus from a survival-of-the-fittest perspective: "It is not the strongest of species that survive, nor the most intelligent, but the most responsive to change." Anthony Muhammad and Luis F. Cruz (2019) note, from a leadership perspective, "Most resistance to change manifests a need that the leader has not met, or a critical investment that a leader has neglected" (p. 19). Angela Duckworth (2016), author of *Grit: The Power of Passion and Perseverance*, writes from a needs perspective, "We change when we need to. Necessity is the mother of adaption" (p. 87). School leaders must embrace the leadership paradox that is the key constant in our work: change is inevitable, growth is optional, so we must embrace the consistency of change and seize the opportunity for growth.

Confrontation vs. Support

In the third edition of *Learning by Doing: A Handbook for Professional Learning Communities at Work*, Richard DuFour, Rebecca DuFour, Robert Eaker, Thomas W. Many, and Mike Mattos (2016) emphasize the leader's role in addressing conflict within schools. DuFour et al. (2016) write:

> Confrontation will typically be the responsibility of the leader (that is, principal or administrator) to communicate what is important and valued by demonstrating a willingness to confront when app-ropriate. Nothing will destroy the credibility of a leader faster than an unwillingness to address an obvious violation of what the orga-nization contends is vital. It is possible to be tough minded and adamant about protecting purpose and priorities while also being tender with people. (p. 213)

In their book *Time for Change*, Muhammad and Cruz (2019) contend, "Leaders' direct or indirect refusal to address adult behavior limits improvement" (p. 87). Muhammad and Cruz (2019) bring into focus the necessary skill of confrontation and accountability within an organization: "Transformational leaders need to create a culture of accountability; however, equally important is the skill set that leaders must be prepared to use so they can hold individuals directly accountable if they fail to hold themselves accountable" (p. 86). A leader's ability to confront incongruences or inconsistencies within the organization underscores what the organization values and considers sacred.

In *Supportive Accountability: How to Inspire People and Improve Performance*, author Sylvia Melena (2018) makes the case for supportive leadership as a crucial ingredient for successful teams. Melena (2018) outlines three pillars that accentuate support for employees: (1) trust, (2) effective communication, and (3) empowerment. The three pillars are embedded with characteristics such as caring, honesty, fairness, and promise keeping. These supportive constructs strengthen the relationship between leaders and teams.

The prospect of balancing confrontation and support may be daunting for some school leaders. However, by furthering awareness and understanding of this paradox, leaders will be better equipped to foster healthy school cultures through a merger of the confrontation and support constructs.

Visible vs. Invisible

Steve Zuieback (2012), author of *Leadership Practices for Challenging Times: Principles, Skills and Processes that Work*, is an expert consultant in the areas of leadership, creative planning, team development, and facilitation skills for education systems. Zuieback has helped countless organizations change course to systems with merit and sustainability; he is a true master at making the invisible visible for teams. His work consistently highlights Margaret Wheatley's (1992) Six-Circle Model as a key driver for whole-system transformation. Zuieback's work with leaders—specifically Sanger's leadership—helped shed light as to why true system change begins with deeper awareness on the part of individuals and teams. While there are several adaptations of Wheatley's model, we will use the Six-Circle Model shown in figure 1.1.

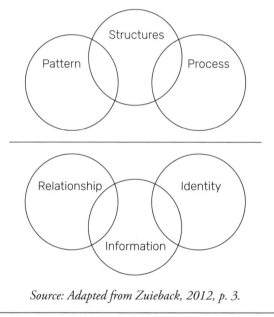

Source: Adapted from Zuieback, 2012, p. 3.

Figure 1.1: Wheatley's (1992) Six-Circle Model.

Above the Green Line

In Wheatley's (1992) model, her research asserts that most organizations approach issues in one or more of the three circles "above the green line"—structures, process, and pattern. Structures, patterns, and processes include short- and long-term strategic plans, schedules, and personnel assignments, as well as goals and objectives. As Zuieback (2012) explains, "The 'hallucination' was that if you changed the structure of the organization—assigned people to have the primary responsibility for a key initiative—the organization would then positively respond to the change" (p. 2). Wheatley's research found that it was not the circles above that elicited change; rather, it was the circles below the green line.

Additional research reinforced the notion that structural change alone is not sufficient for sustainable change. The following passage brings into focus two reasons as to why structural change is popular, but by itself does not foster healthy organizational culture. Richard DuFour and Robert J. Marzano (2011), authors of *Leaders of Learning*, quote Collins (2009) as saying:

> We believe there are two answers to Hattie's question of why schools so often invest so much effort and energy into structural changes that have little impact on student achievement. The first is that structural changes are easy to make. You can change the structure by fiat. The second reason for popularity of structural tweaking is because it allows educators to convey the illusion of change. Reorganizing and restructuring can create a false sense that you are actually doing something productive. Changing the structure or moving boxes around on the organizational chart won't change the culture and too often serve the strategies for avoiding the brutal facts. (p. 173)

Below the Green Line

Contrary to what was originally thought by organizational leaders, Wheatley's (1992) research notes that the organization success was actually dependent upon the information, relationship, and identity factors—those below the green line. Zuieback (2012) asserts:

> Information is like oxygen—when people don't have enough they fall asleep, panic, shut down, hallucinate and eventually die. When information is abundant, rumors decrease, people focus on what is important, have a greater sense of security in knowing what is actually going on in the organization, and get more creative in their ideas, strategies, and solutions. (p. 3)

Relationships represented the organization's value of the physical and emotional health of people. Trust and commitment lead to powerful results. One of the unique nuances in Wheatley's (1992) model was that "relationships occurred not only between people, but between programs, departments, and organizations (connections)" (p. 4). The last of the three circles is identity. Zuieback (2012) refers to organizational identity this way: "Human beings are meaning-seekers. Our actions are completely driven by beliefs, values, and identity. Organizations that provide abundant opportunities to find meaning around their individual and collective work demonstrate significantly improved results" (p. 4).

REFLECTION QUESTIONS

At this point, stop to consider the paradoxes and research mentioned in the previous sections. Take a moment to answer the following questions to help create further awareness for your own team and organizational collective efficacy.

1. What *conditions* do you need to create to develop clarity around the identity of your team or organization?

2. What *questions* do you need to ask to uncover hidden beliefs and perceptions about how your team or organization shares information and builds collaboration structures?

3. What *psychological or social barriers* exist that may deter your team or organization from developing relationships (connections)?

Now that you have considered these questions in relation to your own organization, we will share with you the leadership lessons that Sanger learned in their experience of building culture to enhance collective efficacy.

Leadership Lessons on Culture

In this section, we present to the reader our learnings from both the challenge story we experienced at Sanger Unified School District and the research previously presented. We attempt to bring together the challenge, the paradoxes we shared, and what the research asks us to consider in specific examples.

The leadership lessons we discuss in this section are:

- Balance learning and doing
- Balance above the green line and below the green line

Balance Learning and Doing

Sanger's leaders made a fundamental discovery as part of embracing the BTGL model. What they experienced was conflict between designing direction for teams while at the same time building relationships, information, and identity. They discovered that giving the "charge" to a direction doesn't build the BTGL model. Rather, in order for change to occur, balanced leadership needed to embrace a "learning by doing" approach (DuFour et al., 2016) to the work. Leaders didn't need to learn in isolation and then give the order for the "charge"; rather, leaders and teachers needed to learn *together*. In order for leaders and teams to learn, they need time, resources, and autonomy to process new concepts and ask questions without judgment. Teams also need permission to explore, investigate, and practice new methods and apply new approaches. DuFour et al. (2016) note:

> Perhaps the greatest insight we have gained in our work with school districts in the United States and throughout the world is that organizations that take the plunge and actually begin doing the work of a PLC develop their capacity to help all students learn at high levels far more effectively than schools that spend years *preparing* to become PLCs through reading or even training. (p. 23)

To capture the essence of this change principle, Michael Fullan and Joanne Quinn (2016) argue that educators must move quickly from conversations about mission and vision to action because "it is learning by purposeful doing that counts most" (p. 21).

Sanger's learning-by-doing approach enabled teams to build new beliefs and perceptions that then fostered conditions that enhanced competence and capacity. Teachers became more authentic in sharing experiences and challenges because what were once viewed as failures and weaknesses were reframed as *learning experiences*. For example, in their collaborative teams, teachers challenged each other's beliefs and practices. You heard statements such as, "We have to stay together on our pacing" and "We all agreed to bring data; why aren't we all able to do this?" The statements were examples of a new beginning, a new culture that was fostering team efficacy in a new way.

Learning by doing brought about some hard learning experiences, such as the resignation of the English teacher who believed fellow teachers slashed his tires, and several confrontational exchanges between staffers and leaders who had tremendous pride and long-held beliefs about how business should be done. However, with these new discoveries, leaders planted their flag in the learning-by-doing model, which required them to conduct action-centered research on learning together and made strategic planning secondary. The learning-by-doing and action-centered research (DuFour, DuFour, Eaker, & Many, 2006) was Sanger's spark for mobilizing the PLC process and paved the way for transformative change.

Cultural changes included a new school board that prioritized student learning and collaboration as well as a district leadership team committed to collective decision making. This gave birth to new ideas and a new reality for teams. It helped provide a visible pathway that aligned the current reality and practices to the cultural transformation the organization aspired to create.

Balance Above the Green Line and Below the Green Line

Using the BTGL model essentially created a blueprint for behavior expectations and reset the standard for how people were treated within the Sanger Unified organization. The BTGL model also planted the seed for leaders to consider seeing the work—the good, the bad, and the ugly—through balanced leadership. This BTGL model provided leaders with a refreshed view of organizational system change by teaching them how to embrace the true underpinnings of their work. The renewed perspective allowed teams to be more cognizant of countless paradoxes that exist in the world of team efficacy. However, teams had to be ready, willing, and open to seeing the balance.

The primary lesson learned in building a culture to enhance collective team efficacy is that all successful change starts in the context of identity. Leaders came to learn, through research and experience, that identity is equivalent to the behaviors of the organization. Leaders had historically tried different approaches, from listing norms on agendas and defining collective commitments to having teams outline their own missions, visions, values, and goals, in the hope of making a greater connection to the work. These leadership actions created little change in our organizational culture due to the entrenched dysfunctionality of the system. Likewise, they failed to translate into the ultimate goal of collective team efficacy. Leaders had to learn to ask different questions. Under those conditions, leaders needed to find examples or models on how to create changes in team behaviors. The PLC process led leaders to ask the question, "What do highly collaborative teams do?" Clearly *defining* the behaviors allowed leaders to clearly *identify* the actions of highly collaborative teams.

District work in the context of information was much more practical, but just as meaningful. Leaders learned the profound difference between highly effective teams and highly ineffective teams. Simply put, highly effective teams discussed successes and failures with honesty and transparency. Ineffective teams tended to dismiss low student performance and failures while blaming others or circumstances for the shortfalls. The past organization had learned to successfully hide its failures, ignore results, and point at users in the system for failed outcomes. Those identified as users could be the teacher, principal, superintendent, school board, or, unfortunately at times, students and families.

Leaders already understood the importance of frequency, focus, and clarity around information as crucial ingredients to building a positive organizational culture. However, there was an interesting nuance regarding information sharing that was counterintuitive for leaders. It had previously been widely assumed that a leader's role was to always place a positive spin on information, especially student achievement data, primarily to avoid feelings of defeat or humiliation for teams. However, the information from Wheatley's (1992) model asks leaders and teams to reconsider the *how* and *why* of information sharing. Leaders had to learn to balance optimism without giving a false positive to teams. This meant that leaders needed to be mindful enough to negotiate positive framing of information while being honest about, and sometimes uncomfortable with, the current reality or truth. Leaders learned that "sugar-coating" was not in the best interest of the organization or teams; rather, information sharing was an opportunity to empower individuals through transparent, open, and honest communication.

In addition to the value of identity and information, leaders learned another powerful lesson in attempting to create a culture that fostered collective efficacy. This lesson was embedded in relationships. In her book, *Collective Efficacy: How Educators' Beliefs Impact Student Learning*, Jenni Donohoo (2017) notes that "change is dependent on the relationships within it" (p. 55). Donohoo (2017) also references Wheatley's (1992) work and asserts that "in organizations, real power and energy are generated through relationships—the patterns of relationships and the capacities to form them are more important than tasks, functions, roles, and positions" (p. 55). This deeper understanding of the power of fostering relationships was initially absent from Sanger's organizational framework. However, with this revelation, the magnitude of relationship building became embedded in the hearts and minds of leaders and teams.

Conclusion: Connecting Culture to Collective Teacher Efficacy

The Sanger Unified organization learned that culture had to be the unequivocal driving force for change. Teams learned that if they embraced the concept of below the green line as the nucleus of culture, then moving structures, strategies, and operations would presumably come with ease. Anthony Muhammad (2018), one of the most sought-after educational consultants in the world, put his own twist on a popular leadership mantra when he re-emphasized the importance of leaders fostering collaborative cultures, stating, "Culture eats strategy for breakfast, operational excellence for lunch, and everything else in between." If organizations truly wish to build collective team efficacy and healthy school cultures, then leaders must embrace the myriad of paradoxes, unpredictable challenges, and meaningful research when leading transformation.

Next Steps

In this section, we provide the reader with some simple next steps associated with the learnings from the readings. You may take these steps either individually or as a team.

- Use the 1–5–10 assessment tool shown in the reproducible "1–5–10 Assessment Tool: Culture" (page 30) to assess the culture (relationships, information, and identity) within your school or organization.

- Upon completion of the 1–5–10 scale, complete the reproducible "Keep, Start, Stop, or Improve Chart" (page 31) to determine a focus area and generate ideas and next steps for improving collective team efficacy. This reproducible also includes a completed example.

1-5-10 Assessment Tool: Culture

Assess and score your organization on each of the ten statements, with 1 being the lowest and 10 being the highest. Then calculate your total score.

Relationships	Score
Relationships are more important than *tasks*, *functions*, *roles*, or *position*.	1-5-10
Relationships reflect *respect*, *trust*, and *integrity*.	1-5-10
Relationships are *deeply valued* and considered *sacred*.	1-5-10
Relationships *equally value* individuals' *personal* and *professional lives*.	1-5-10
Information	**Score**
Information is shared frequently and considered *honest* and *transparent*.	1-5-10
Information is shared frequently and centered around *student outcomes*.	1-5-10
Information is shared frequently for the primary purpose of *improving collective teacher practices* and is never considered a *"gotcha"* or used to take staff by surprise.	1-5-10
Identity	**Score**
The identity of the organization is *always* reflected in the *mission*, *vision*, *values*, and *goals*.	1-5-10
The identity of the organization is *always* reflected in individual or team *beliefs*.	1-5-10
The identity of the organization is *always* reflected in individual or team *behaviors*.	1-5-10
Total points (maximum possible: 100)	

Collective Efficacy in a PLC at Work® © 2021 Solution Tree Press

SolutionTree.com • Visit **go.SolutionTree.com/PLCbooks** to download this free reproducible.

Keep, Start, Stop, or Improve Chart

Based on the 1–5–10 scales, which areas pose the greatest challenge for your team—relationships, information, or identity? Use the Keep, Start, Stop, or Improve Chart to guide your teams' conversations to improve one element in each area your team identifies.

Relationships: Describe the specific challenge area.	Keep, Start, Stop, or Improve	How Will We Monitor Progress?
	What Do We Need To: **Keep Doing?** **Start Doing?** **Stop Doing?** **Improve?**	
Information: Describe the specific challenge area.	Keep, Start, Stop, or Improve	How Will We Monitor Progress?
	What Do We Need To: **Keep Doing?** **Start Doing?** **Stop Doing?** **Improve?**	
Identity: Describe the specific challenge area.	Keep, Start, Stop, or Improve	How Will We Monitor Progress?
	What Do We Need To: **Keep Doing?** **Start Doing?** **Stop Doing?** **Improve?**	

page 1 of 2

Collective Efficacy in a PLC at Work® © 2021 Solution Tree Press

SolutionTree.com • Visit **go.SolutionTree.com/PLCbooks** to download this free reproducible.

Relationships: Describe the specific challenge area.	Keep, Start, Stop, or Improve	How Will We Monitor Progress?
Relationships are more important than tasks, functions, roles, or position.	**What Do We Need To:** **Keep Doing?** Keep expectations high, even for little things, making sure we are completing assignments for our team on time. **Start Doing?** Administrators and staff need to have conversations around why certain compliance documents, tasks, and functions are so important and what can be done to better organize the department. **Stop Doing?** Stop putting fear in staff around deadlines and compliance. **Improve?** We need to improve gratitude and being more intentional with our appreciation of how hard everyone is working.	At the end of every month, administrators will meet with teams to explain what is coming up for the next month, what needs to be completed, and any support that might be provided as well as deadline dates for tasks associated with upcoming priorities.

page 2 of 2

Collective Efficacy in a PLC at Work® © 2021 Solution Tree Press

SolutionTree.com • Visit **go.SolutionTree.com/PLCbooks** to download this free reproducible.

BUILDING PURPOSE TO ENHANCE COLLECTIVE EFFICACY

"To inspire starts with clarity of WHY."

—Simon Sinek

Rachel Eells (2011), in her dissertation titled *Meta-Analysis of the Relationship Between Collective Teacher Efficacy and Student Achievement*, writes, "Together, people can accomplish that which one person cannot. Social action depends on a belief that a group can effect change. Collective efficacy helps people realize their shared destiny" (p. 51). Building purpose to enhance collective efficacy for Sanger would require leaders to examine exactly "Why do we exist?" (DuFour et al., 2010). To answer this, leaders were compelled to reflect on their personal and collective journeys and draw on examples from the past.

One of the greatest visionaries of modern time was Dr. Martin Luther King Jr. In his famous speech on August 28, 1963, during the March on Washington, King brought a powerful vision infused with greater purpose as he stood before his fellow Americans. "I have a dream!" were the words etched in the annals of history. He didn't say, "I have a strategy," or "I have a program," or "I have a schedule." The people in attendance, physically or otherwise, were inspired for change because he presented a shared destiny and delivered it heart-to-heart with extraordinary belief and undying conviction. The *why* of Dr. King's message was a higher calling, a higher purpose, that connected millions of people to something greater than themselves.

To this end, collective efficacy begins and ends with beliefs: the beliefs of individuals and the beliefs within teams. Decades of research have continued to make the clear determinations that "beliefs about ourselves, others, and how the world works predict how high we set our life goals and whether we actually succeed in achieving them" (Caproni, 2017, p. 27).

Purpose is bonded to collective efficacy because it actually resides within our convictions, perceptions, and beliefs; beliefs not only about why we exist but about our competence and capability to succeed. If our individual or collective purpose is perceived as miniscule or insignificant, to what degree of motivation does that serve? How much potential may be deterred or inhibited because schools lack a higher purpose?

In this chapter, we highlight the story of Jefferson Elementary and the experiences they shared when transforming themselves from one of the lowest performing schools in the district and state to one of the highest performing. This experience occurred between 2000 and 2010 and focused on building the staff's understanding of their true purpose.

The Challenge: Jefferson Elementary

Jefferson Elementary, founded in 1955, is a small K–6 elementary school just inside the city limits of Sanger. In 2001, Jefferson was struggling to achieve meaningful academic outcomes for students. Located on the east side of town, across the railroad tracks, Jefferson's surrounding area had a high degree of poverty, gang activity, and crime. Standard in the Jefferson community were high-density apartments, low-income housing, high populations of English learners, and a high percentage of socioeconomically disadvantaged families. It was a harsh reality that large numbers of students in the Jefferson area had family members either involved or formerly involved in gangs, drugs, or incarceration.

Many struggles that plagued the community were outside the Jefferson staff's locus of control. However, what was in their control was maintaining pride and honoring traditions that lifted the spirits of students, staff, and community. Amidst such a poverty-stricken neighborhood, Jefferson and its facilities were immaculate. It didn't take visitors long to figure out why. Albert Mendoza, who retired in 2021 after forty-nine years of service, had been the custodian at Jefferson since 1972 and was a respected pillar in the community. In fact, many of the staff at Jefferson had many years of service at the school. Many teachers had students whose parents had also been their students years earlier. Because of the pride in the school and longevity of staff, which equated to strong relationships with the community, the school was essentially off-limits to vandalism, graffiti, and theft. The school community, regardless of the hardships it faced, took pride in their school, and it showed in the care of the facilities as well as in the community's protection of its staff.

By 2001, the state of California was moving forward with the legislation surrounding No Child Left Behind (NCLB). The state had rolled out scores for schools by assigning schools a score through an academic performance index (API). In Jefferson's case, its initial API score was 456 API out of a possible 1,000, placing it in the bottom 2 percent of schools in the state (www.cde.ca.gov; data no longer available). As the state transitioned to the new federal accountability model through NCLB, it began to identify schools in need of greater accountability, which could include administrative or school staff changes. As a result of the new focus on data, many in the educational system identified Jefferson as one of the lowest-performing schools in the state of California. Specifically, Jefferson was identified through NCLB's similar-schools ranking as a 1 out of 10 when compared to *all schools* and *similar schools' demographics* across the state (www.cde.ca.gov; data no longer available). Within NCLB, the bottom schools in the state of California were beginning to feel the mounting pressure of school rankings as well as the public display of achievement data that would signify the success or failure of the educators teaching the students.

Despite the mounting pressure of sanctions, Jefferson was still a happy family, with staff and faculty who loved their students like their own, and cared deeply about the community. As a result of the new NCLB requirements and penalties, parents and families could opt out of attending Jefferson and could ask the district to fund and pay for the transportation of their children to go to another, more successful school within or outside of the district. So how many parents requested a transfer with this new option? Not one! What Jefferson had was a school and community who were feeling "good" but doing "bad."

Despite these rankings, by 2000, the situation at Jefferson had minimally changed. The change incentives were there—teams were offered professional improvement, and NCLB had now publicly anointed Jefferson as one of the lowest-ranked and lowest-performing schools in California, leading to humiliation and sometimes suffocating pressure—but nothing had actually made enough of an impact to change the school's overall test results. In an effort to change course, Jefferson's leadership took a different approach. At the opening staff meeting in 2001, leadership posed the following questions, adapted from the PLC process, for staff to consider.

- Why do we exist?
- How do we prove why we exist?
- How do we showcase our students' abilities to the rest of the world?

These questions helped shape a deeper level of conversation and discussion among staff and provided opportunities for staff to open up about their core beliefs, convictions, and, more importantly, assumptions about the students and the community. The questions forced honest reflection from individuals and teams with regard to efforts, expectations, and commitment. Conflicts initially surfaced from emotional trigger points and transitioned to unfiltered, genuine dialogue around a unifying collective purpose. The respect and dignity of the staff were always treated with great care. The Jefferson staff's love for their students was unquestionable. However, the *why* had to be put front and center. The staff needed a greater purpose for why they existed in light of the students and the community.

With that call, leaders stopped speaking to the minds of staff and instead spoke to their hearts. These conversations were gently infused with genuineness, grace, and an emotional delivery that fostered clarity of purpose (the *why*). And it was collective clarity of purpose that changed the trajectory of Jefferson, as shown in figure 2.1. As a result, it also changed their identity.

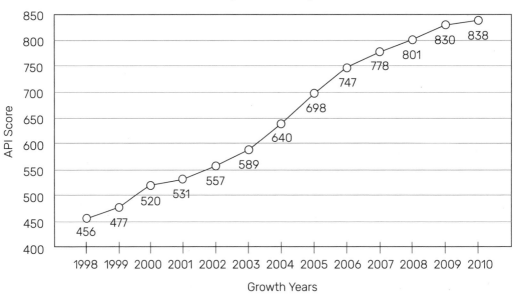

Jefferson API Growth
(1998–2010)

Source: California Department of Education, n.d.

Figure 2.1: Jefferson Elementary academic performance index (1998–2010).

The Change

So, what did Jefferson do to move from being one of the lowest-performing schools in the state, with an API of 456 in 1998, to becoming one of the highest-performing schools in the district and one of the most compelling school turnaround stories in the state, with an API of 838, by 2010? There were three distinctions, inspired by the PLC process's three big ideas, that were paramount in Jefferson's transformation. Leadership and staff:

1. Stopped looking at the scoreboard and started chasing the vision

2. Made a monumental shift in thinking so that learning was the priority, not teaching

3. Articulated that a change in API benefitted how the world viewed their students

When Jefferson staff stopped looking at the scoreboard (namely, the NCLB test scores) as a judgment of them and started looking at it as a judgment of their students' abilities, it ignited a passion to prove to the world that this judgment was wrong. The vision of students being able to succeed in life redefined test scores as secondary to a greater purpose. That shift placed student learning front and center. If the staff were going to change the district, city, and state view of their students, then the staff had to strive to empower students to demonstrate what they learned on the test in order to achieve the vision for what the staff hoped they could accomplish.

What connected to the heart of the work was that the state API rankings were a judgment by the state to the rest of the world about their students' abilities, capabilities, and futures. Demonstrating student learning was the only way to prove that Jefferson students could surpass the expectations of the world and meet the expectations that staff already had. The reframing and refocusing of test scores as a secondary means to a vision ignited a powerful, symbolic representation that united the school around the right call to action. The remarkable improvement in performance served as a revelation to the world that Jefferson's purpose was meaningful. Jefferson eventually became a lighthouse for researchers, funders, and those who desperately wanted to understand the *how* of school turnaround.

PRACTITIONER PERSPECTIVE

"We never would have ever imagined that Jefferson would have achieved such improved student outcomes. We never were motivated by the district's idea of chasing test scores; we were motivated by a cause of using the test to show everyone how special our kids are."

—Kellee Barsotti
Fifth-Grade Teacher,
Jefferson Elementary (1984–present)

Leadership Paradoxes

Initially, district and site leaders all across Sanger faced the new challenge of creating the conditions necessary to connect teams to a greater purpose, as in the case of Jefferson. This isn't to say that teachers didn't have individual causes that motivated them, or that leaders were somehow acting as saviors for school sites. Rather, leadership understood that capturing purpose unquestionably would be a collective endeavor. The truth was that the new leaders possessed such a pure, powerful devotion to "doing what was best for kids" that it was critical to ensure the same undeniable passion and belief were expressed by all throughout the organization. The mission for leaders and teams was to tap into the invisible spirit, that humanistic side of people, the place where inspiration lives—where the message speaks directly to the heart. Leaders would need both authenticity and the wherewithal to connect with teams and unearth a deeper meaning of purpose.

The nuances of purpose would need to be properly understood if leaders were to gain clarity for the organization. Leaders needed adequate time to reflect, interpret, and analyze their own professional purpose before ever beginning to consider their ability to access the collective purpose of teams. Awakening the organization's higher calling requires leaders to sort through the buried contradictions of leadership to uncover the truths of schools.

The specific leadership paradoxes Sanger's leadership encountered when building purpose to enhance collective efficacy were:

- Feeling good vs. doing badly
- Questions vs. answers
- Significance vs. contribution
- Limbic system vs. the neocortex

Feeling Good vs. Doing Badly

The "feeling good, doing badly" paradox was a prevalent theme throughout the district. Prevalent because teachers and leaders were highly motivated, were hardworking, and understood the district mission to raise achievement scores, but to no avail. Ongoing district and school site formative assessment data simply did not reflect the anticipated uptick in student learning as anticipated. The "feeling good, doing badly" paradox was real; however, all teachers and leaders may not have been fully aware of the difference. Leaders acknowledged the obvious discrepancy between having positive feelings and achieving negative results within their schools but realized it was difficult to articulate in words. In addition, leaders noticed that the cultural dynamic of some schools was to simply accept the "feeling good, doing badly" paradox, and they wanted to find out if staff were even aware of the paradox. Additionally, the origins of "feeling good, doing badly" would need to be vetted out by leadership and staff while navigating the process with both delicacy and respect. The "feeling good, doing badly" context would require a sort of gentle relentlessness, a balanced leadership approach when attempting to rationalize changes that needed to be made to the organization for the sake of purpose.

Finally, leaders struggled not only with this paradox but even more so with being responsible for delivering the message that their collective best was thus far not good enough. Specifically, confronting the reality of schools doing their best given the current beliefs and supports in place would require a heavy-handed reality check with an even stronger voice and compelling vision for what was possible. Such a task was complicated and required a unique set of leadership abilities. Leaders worried about the high probability that bringing to light the discrepancy of "feeling good, doing badly" could create the perception of disrespect or degradation, potentially breaking the spirit of schools that were naturally humble by circumstance, yet enormously prideful in traditions. No leader wished to become the enemy of the team they were entrusted to lead.

Questions vs. Answers

Another leadership paradox—questions vs. answers—posed a different set of challenges for leaders. At first glance, questions and answers seem fairly routine for school organizations: leaders ask questions, teams provide answers, and vice versa. However, when considering the massive overhaul of low-performing school structures and protocols along with creating a new way of conducting business, it was nothing of the sort. Historically, district leaders had shared important, but somewhat routine, less critical information regarding schedules, duties, and events. The district had prioritized the management of the schools as a key indicator of positive performance for leaders. However, now that the school organizations were seeking to inspire change through the power of purpose around student learning, leaders would need to stretch themselves to create the conditions necessary to embrace a heartfelt dialogue with the intent to connect to teams. Better yet, leaders would have to become instructional leaders, not just site managers, and the district would have to prioritize this through their own actions and behaviors. It was obvious at some point that no number of agendas, schedules, or event calendars was going to pull schools like Jefferson from the established habit of low expectations and poor beliefs. Only a deep commitment to beliefs and convictions supporting a clear purpose that valued student learning would be reflected in school and student performance.

Leaders could only create these conditions through thoughtful questioning and skilled facilitation. Balanced leadership in this context would require much bigger, much deeper questions that evoked raw emotions from teams. In theory, the PLC process would create the right conditions and serve as a catalyst to fundamentally reset the organization's axis around a greater purpose. However, what caused apprehension for leaders was being put in a position of vulnerability as facilitators.

To do this right, leaders would need to create the conditions necessary to connect viscerally and emotionally with teams through grander questions that couldn't be answered with simple responses. Leaders needed to inspire teams with questions that forced them to look deeper into the collective psyche while delivering a fundamental message with precision, purpose, and heartfelt sentiment.

Significance vs. Contribution

There was a districtwide struggle to capture the real *significance* of teams, given the history of poor achievement results and the giant wall of status quo. PLC members could capture significance through various means; indeed, simple acknowledgements and recognition serve as excellent validation of teachers' and leaders' efforts for their individual or collective accomplishments.

Conversely, there was also a districtwide struggle for site leaders to capture the essence and importance of framing the staff's work as a *contribution* to the greater purpose. Contribution meant that PLC members needed to concede to the deeper purpose of their work—the greater good. Contribution also meant that PLC members would need to give selflessly, focusing less on independent accolades and more on team interdependence.

The significance vs. contribution paradox revealed the desperate need for district and site leaders to find the *why* for teams. Leaders were challenged to help facilitate a deeper dive to define significance and contribution for individual staff and teams, while capturing the overarching themes of their collective purpose. The facilitation of these experiences would require leaders to increase their own self-awareness and mental framework, through in-depth reflection and processing.

Limbic System vs. the Neocortex

District and site leadership faced the challenge of connecting with teams both analytically and emotionally. Therefore, leadership sought to explore how to balance these two somewhat opposing approaches and find better ways to truly connect to teams. This led some leaders to consider research associated with brain function—specifically research on the limbic system and the neocortex. First, the limbic system is the part of the brain that deals with three important functions: emotions, memories, and stimulation. Within the limbic system is a specific region of the brain called the amygdala, which triggers action. This region controls the part of the brain that processes fear, triggers anger, and motivates us. It alerts us to danger and activates the fight or flight response.

In stark contrast to the limbic system, the neocortex "is involved in higher functions such as sensory perception, generation of motor commands, spatial reasoning, conscious thought, and in humans, language" (ScienceDaily.com, n.d.). Further, "the neocortex is a complex structure—dozens of cells, intricate connectivity patterns, and multiple layers" (HumanMemory.net, 2020). There is a unique function of the neocortex worth noting—it stores information about the structure of the environment and builds connections between the different parts of the brain based on the mental frameworks of these structures. This means that individuals and teams create their own framework based on how they perceive their environment, contexts, and situations.

The organizational leadership, in this change journey, challenged leaders to negotiate the two regions of the brain when communicating, collaborating, and attempting to build collective purpose. Leaders were accustomed to speaking and conducting business with a sort of "neocortex stance" that was easily accessible for all leaders regardless of skill set or experience. However, leadership found that school leaders who possessed a natural way of connecting and motivating teams—an X factor, if you will—tended to experience more success in rallying teams around a clear cause. A leader's innate ability to inspire and connect with people and clearly establish a purpose for teams was hard to define with words (a characteristic associated with the limbic region). This dilemma led leaders to further explore how to connect teams with a greater purpose.

Leadership Research

The following research helps to complement and build on the paradoxes Sanger's leadership discovered in the challenge. The paradox of discoveries leads us to consider research that either complements or challenges what we learned.

We reviewed research for each of the paradoxes described in the previous section:

- Feeling good vs. doing badly
- Questions vs. answers
- Significance vs. contribution
- Limbic system vs. the neocortex

Feeling Good vs. Doing Badly

The struggle to understand why the "feeling good, doing badly" paradox existed led leaders to a psychology term: *cognitive dissonance.* In 1954, Leon Festinger first introduced the theory of cognitive dissonance to describe a psychological phenomenon that typically occurs when a person holds contradictory beliefs, ideas, or values and, as a result, experiences psychological stress. Similarly, psychologist Saul McLeod (2018) defines cognitive dissonance as referring to "a situation involving conflicting attitudes, beliefs, or behaviors. Cognitive dissonance produces a feeling of mental discomfort leading to an alteration in one of the attitudes, beliefs, or behaviors to reduce the discomfort and restore balance."

According to these definitions, there is supposed to be an obvious "stressor"—a discrepancy or misalignment for individuals—that leads to discomfort and, ultimately, to a person changing their beliefs or actions to restore psychological equilibrium.

However, the nuance that district and site leaders faced, especially with Jefferson Elementary, was there was no cognitive dissonance. There was no discomfort with "feeling good, doing badly" because they rejected the "doing badly" label altogether. No one was walking around with their head down and tail tucked. Leaders found that staffers' feelings and actions were actually aligned because, in their minds, they were truly maximizing their potential given the historical and cultural circumstances of the community and staff capacity at the time. Using this research, leaders must learn to consider the gentle introduction of the discrepancy between the current reality and new vision, and then thoughtfully articulate a greater purpose with a relentless enthusiasm for change that creates a degree of discomfort—enough to create change—with the current reality.

Questions vs. Answers

Widely considered one of the top leadership authorities in the world, John C. Maxwell (2014), in his book *Good Leaders Ask Great Questions*, emphasizes:

> Life is a journey, one in which we seek to find our way and make a difference. In fact, the word question is derived from the Latin root word *quaerere* meaning "ask" or "seek." It has the same root word as "quest." Sometimes the questions come from others and sometimes the questions are ones we ask. Either way, the answers mark us. (p. 15)

Leaders unfamiliar with asking important questions and receiving deep answers now had to rethink the art of casting questions in relation to purpose. In addition, the district leaders needed to consider Maxwell's "quest" metaphor in relation to the district's new path.

With this newly reframed mindset, organizational leadership sought to anchor teams with a set of questions that provided a pathway—an exemplar of what to ask. For this exemplar, Sanger turned to the PLC process (DuFour et al., 2016). According to DuFour et al. (2016), within the four pillars of a PLC (mission, vision, values, and goals) are specific questions for teams to use to spark discussion around organizational identity and purpose. These questions include:

- Why do we exist?

- What must our school become to accomplish our purpose?

- How must we behave to achieve our vision?

- How will we mark our progress? (DuFour et al., 2016, p. 39)

These four pillars helped shape and align our organizational messaging with a powerful purpose and served as meaningful guideposts for leaders, setting the path for district transformation.

In regard to answers, however, we found an interesting nuance in the research. Although the concept of "answers" seemed straightforward, Maxwell (2014) had an interesting take for leaders. Rather than first seeking answers from individuals or teams, Maxwell (2014) proposes listening with intention and authenticity as the key ingredient for leaders, asserting, "Good leaders listen, learn, and then lead" (p. 49). Truly listening meant that leaders need to resist the fast pace and whirlwind of school life. In order to accomplish this sort of organic process of being present, leaders needed to adopt more of a "learn to be still" approach, as the legendary Eagles classic rock song states (Henley & Lynch, 1994). "Learning to be still" for leaders meant giving teams undivided attention, noticing nuances, empathizing, and wholeheartedly seeking to connect.

Given the context of typical high-pressure leadership, time constraints, and the need to get through the vast amounts of information and initiatives, "learning to be still" may be considered a pipe dream. However, the research reinforced the importance of leaders being able to intimately connect with teams by eliminating distraction and focusing on genuineness, absent judgment or fear.

This collective awareness and listening research helped leaders establish deeper rapport and meaningful connection within teams and across the organization. Maxwell's (2014) research shows us that great leaders facilitate deeper dialogue and emote challenges through a balance of purposeful questioning and intentional listening. Through the research, we found that if organizational leaders are going to pose grander questions, we needed to be ready to not just listen but to truly hear, embrace, and reflect the message. DuFour et al.'s (2016) PLC process provides the framework for leaders to ask questions while Maxwell (2014) provides the new paradigm for authentic listening.

Significance vs. Contribution

It is somewhat undisputed that school organizations are made up of individuals whose primary purpose is to contribute to the greater good; that is the essence of being an educator. Educators are inherently contributing to the future by attempting to enhance the lives of students through teaching and learning. In his best-selling book *The Eighth Habit: From Effectiveness to Greatness*, Stephen R. Covey (2004) asserts, "Deep within each one of us there is an inner longing to live a life of greatness and contribution—to really matter, to really make a difference" (p. 28). All, or at least most, educators do want to make a difference in their professional lives. In *The Multiplier Effect: Tapping the Genius Inside Our Schools*, Liz Wiseman, Lois Allen, and Elise Foster (2013) further the case by saying, "When leaders connect people's natural passion and native genius to big opportunities, those people are used at their highest point of contribution" (p. 34). However, although district leadership had the best of intentions, there were characteristics in the approach that resembled that of a car salesman. Leaders would typically cast a desperate pitch of a vision or initiative, much like a car salesman trying to meet a quota. Leaders needed to focus less on the car salesman approach and more on connecting to the individual and collective psyche of the organization, using the significance versus contribution paradox. The only way to do this is to honor teams by giving voice to the individuals that make them up. Covey (2004) re-enforces, "Once you've found your voice, the choice to expand your influence, to increase your contribution, is the choice to inspire others to find their voice. Inspire (from Latin *inspirare*) means to breathe life into another" (p. 31). District and site leaders needed to "breathe life" into the organization through consistency and clarity of purpose.

In addition, our leaders found the counterpart to contribution was significance. It is inherently human nature to seek significance. In his book *Man's Search for Meaning*, Viktor E. Frankl (2006) writes, "The true meaning of life is to be discovered in the world rather than within man or his own psyche" (p. 110). This quote by Frankl also reinforces the idea of significance within the leadership paradox. Significance—or meaning, as Frankl states—is to be recognized in the world we operate in, no matter how big or small. Within education settings, significance is attained through individual accolades, honors, and achievements. Significance could also be attained through the collective achievements of collaborative teams. Leaders, however, found a nuance to significance that unlocked a new paradigm for the district. Although individuals and teams naturally or aggressively sought significance, whether publicly stated or not, they were far more inspired when the narrative changed. Chasing personal significance obviously served as a powerful motivator; however, the reframing of personal to collective significance—to serve as the conduit for empowering students to discover their own significance—was invigorating for teams. This was the essence of change needed; teams' need to become significant through contribution was a meaningful research discovery that powered the organization engine moving forward.

Limbic system vs. the Neocortex

Science tells us the limbic system and neocortex help human beings articulate feelings and language, respectively. In his cutting-edge work *Start With Why*, Simon Sinek (2009) distinguishes these two regions of the brain that serve very different functions. Sinek's concept of the Golden Circle forced leaders, regardless of areas of expertise, to rethink their approaches when considering highly effective practices. The Golden Circle describes three areas: (1) the outer layer is the *what*; (2) the middle area is the *how*; and (3) the inner layer is the *why*. Sinek (2009) describes the meaning of the science behind the Golden Circle, asserting:

> Its principles are deeply grounded in the evolution of human be-
> havior. The power of WHY is not opinion, it's biology. If you look at a
> cross-section of the human brain, from the top down, you see that

the levels of The Golden Circle correspond precisely with the three major levels of the brain. (p. 55)

Figure 2.2 compares the three layers of the circle to the basic framework of the brain's limbic system and neocortex.

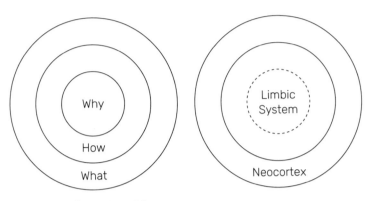

Source: Adapted from Sinek, 2009, p. 56.

Figure 2.2: The Golden Circle compared to the limbic system and neocortex.

Sinek goes on to describe the importance of the limbic system and the neocortex in relation to function. We were hesitant to leave any of Sinek's (2009) description out due to its extreme importance to this particular balanced leadership paradox:

> The newest area of the brain, our *Homo sapiens* brain, is the neocortex, which corresponds with the WHAT level. The neocortex is responsible for rational and analytical thought and language. The middle two sections comprise the limbic brain. The limbic brain is responsible for all of our feelings, such as trust and loyalty. It is responsible for all human behavior and all our decision making, but it has no capacity for language. It is this reason why putting our words into feelings is so hard. (p. 56)

> The heart represents the limbic system, feeling part of the brain, and the mind is the rational, language center. Most companies are quite adept at winning minds; all that is required is a comparison of all the features and benefits. Winning hearts, however, takes more work. The ability to win hearts before minds is not easy. Given the evidence of the natural order of decision-making, I can't help but wonder if the order of the expression "hearts and minds" is a coincidence. Why does no one set out to win minds and hearts? Perhaps our brains are trying to tell us that WHY must come first. (p. 59)

Leaders had to truly appreciate the power of why for collaborative teams. To do this, leaders had to become fully invested to explore and discover their site's deeper purpose, breaking from the traditional standard that upheld a facade to the realities of poor student achievement.

REFLECTION QUESTIONS

At this point, stop to consider the paradoxes and research mentioned in the previous sections. Take a moment to answer the following questions to help create further awareness for your own team and organizational collective efficacy.

1. What *conditions* do you need to create to develop clarity around the purpose of your team or organization?

2. What *questions* do you need to ask to uncover hidden beliefs, convictions, and perceptions about how your team or organization feels about its purpose?

3. What potential *psychological or* team barriers exist that may deter your team or organization from finding purpose?

Now that you have considered these questions in relation to your own organization, we will share with you the leadership lessons that Sanger learned in their experience of building purpose to enhance collective efficacy.

Leadership Lessons on Purpose

In this section, we present to the reader our learnings from both the challenge story we experienced at Sanger Unified School District and the research previously presented. We attempt to bring together the challenge, the paradoxes we shared, and what the research asks us to consider in specific examples.

The leadership lessons we discuss in this section are:

- Speak to the heart
- Achieve transcendence

Speak to the Heart

The Sanger organization learned a profound, overarching lesson during its time of change. Speaking to the heart of individuals and teams brought a synergistic quality that meant more to the organizational culture than all the other structural and systematic approaches combined. Historically, speaking to the minds of individuals and teams about a new vision, purpose, values, and goals was an organizational strength. However, blending concepts with best practices and preparing strategic plans with implementation protocols were all designed to access the cerebral (analytical) part of individuals and teams, not to access human purpose. John C. Maxwell (2005), in his book *The 360° Leader*, echoed those sentiments: "Although vision tells people where they need to go, purpose tells them *why* they should go" (p. 250). Engaging the organization on the topic of purpose compelled leaders to speak to the heart of teams. This required a different, hard-to-define skill set; an authenticity laced with kindness and empathy; and a presence that captivated teams, not with charm but with heartfelt belief. Ultimately, leaders learned that helping teams find the right *why* was the quintessential lynchpin connecting teams to the higher purpose, with an impact that extended far beyond the walls of a classroom.

In his book *HEART! Fully Forming Your Professional Life As a Teacher and Leader*, Timothy D. Kanold (2017) defines the importance of connection and fulfillment in five key areas. These elements—*happiness, engagement, alliances, risk,* and *thought*—help characterize Kanold's *heartprint*. The five *HEART!* elements are "essential to deeper connection to your work over the lifetime of your professional career" (Kanold, 2017, p. 3). The combination of these elements enhances the leader's ability to connect with teams and communities for the greater good, a higher purpose that extends beyond self. Kanold's framework provided leaders with a virtual master class in the power of connection, and a profound lesson for the organization that would never be taken for granted again: "Authentic purpose speaks to the heart" (Deal & Peterson, 2009, p. 62).

Achieve Transcendence

Transcendence can be defined as exceeding or surpassing usual limits. Transcendence can also be described as beyond and outside the ordinary range of human experience or understanding. But how does this topic apply in a school setting? Well, the truth is that the power of purpose and the concept of transcendence touch every facet of the school organization. There is no better research on the topic of transcendence than that of Abraham H. Maslow (1954). Maslow was an American psychologist best known for creating the hierarchy of needs, a theory of psychological health predicated on fulfilling innate human needs by priority and culminating in self-actualization. Maslow's hierarchy of needs revolutionized psychology and poured over into business and education settings. However, this powerful tool is still underutilized in educational settings and practices today.

Figure 2.3 displays Maslow's six-level hierarchy. Its levels are: (1) physiology, (2) safety, (3) belonging, (4) esteem within the community, (5) self-actualization, and (6) connection to something greater than self.

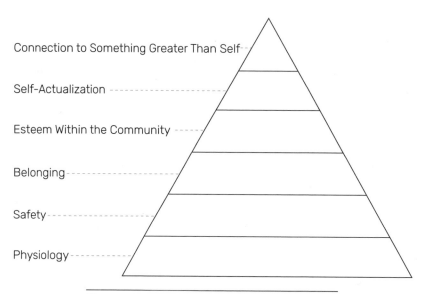

Figure 2.3: Maslow's hierarchy of needs.

Physiology, the lowest level of Maslow's hierarchy, is the most basic of human needs related to comfort (namely, food and water). *Safety*, the second-lowest level on the hierarchy, refers to a sense of order, predictability, fairness, and security (for example, home stability). *Belonging* is a human need that compels us to seek fulfillment and affection in relationships (for example, connection to others). *Esteem within the community* refers to a person's self-concept—the way they see themselves within various contexts (for example, as a contributor, follower, or leader). *Self-actualization* is a need that refers to "the desire to become more and more what one is, to become everything that one is capable of becoming" (Maslow, 1943, p. 382). *Connection to something greater than self* is the highest level of need on Maslow's hierarchy; it is the inclination to fulfill potential with purpose that extends beyond self.

Other experts have reinforced the power of purpose in their experiences and writings. The authors of *Shaping School Culture: Pitfalls, Paradoxes, and Promises*, Terrence E. Deal and Kent D. Peterson (2009), write, "People need a medium that will help people connect viscerally and emotionally with the school's reason for existence, its higher calling" (p. 62). Daniel Pink (2009) describes purpose this way: "The most deeply motivated people hitch their desires to a cause larger than themselves" (p. 133). The bottom line is this: purpose runs deep. If leaders can harness the powerful ability to authentically and wholeheartedly connect with others, and teams reciprocate that same genuineness, then leaders can realize the potential to unlock a higher purpose for organizational transformation.

Conclusion: Connecting Purpose to Collective Efficacy

Purpose is powerful. Through the lens of collective efficacy, the degree of perceived purpose (the *why* for existence) profoundly impacts the perceived degree of competence or capacity. This perception can positively or negatively affect outcomes. In addition, beliefs about collective purpose influence the degree to which individuals or teams persevere and show resilience attributes in the face of adversity.

The absence of purpose can cause a huge imbalance to the collective efficacy ecosystem, negatively affecting motivation and effort expenditure. If organizational purpose is tainted or contrived, the beliefs of individuals and teams will diminish, as will collective efficacy. Leaders who aspire to create and nourish conditions to foster a higher collective purpose may need to be reminded where to begin. As Sinek (2009) so eloquently states, "To inspire starts with clarity of WHY" (p. 66).

Leaders hoping to build purpose to enhance collective efficacy can learn from Sanger's turnaround by understanding and balancing the paradoxes of feeling good versus doing badly, asking deep questions and seeking deep answers, considering significance versus contribution, and appealing to the limbic system as well as the neocortex. We encourage leaders transitioning through change to speak to the heart of those you lead, help teams seek the right *why*, and connect the purpose of teams and the organization to something greater than oneself.

Next Steps

In this section, we provide the reader some simple next steps to take as a team associated with the learnings from the readings.

- Use the reproducible "1–5–10 Assessment Tool: Purpose" (page 50) to assess purpose within your school or organization.

- Use the reproducible "Driving Force Analysis Process" (page 51) to move challenging purpose areas to positive purpose areas.

- Use the "Team Improvement Assessment Questionnaire" reproducible (page 52) up to three times a year to help your team build a clear purpose for their work and improve team efficacy.

1-5-10 Assessment Tool: Purpose

Assess and score each of the ten statements, with 1 being the lowest and 10 being the highest. Then calculate your total score.

Purpose	Score
Purpose is clearly reflected in the team or organization's mission.	1–5–10
Purpose is clearly reflected in the team or organization's vision.	1–5–10
Purpose is clearly reflected in the team or organization's values.	1–5–10
Purpose is clearly reflected in the team or organization's goals.	1–5–10
Complete cohesion exists across teams in owning the fundamental purpose of the organization.	1–5–10
The fundamental purpose of the organization speaks to the heart of individuals and teams.	1–5–10
The fundamental purpose of the organization inherently creates motivation and inspiration to act.	1–5–10
The fundamental purpose of the organization reflects Maslow's highest level of fulfillment: "Connection to something greater than self."	1–5–10
Teams can clearly articulate how they must behave to achieve the purpose.	1–5–10
Teams can clearly articulate "why" the team or organization exists.	1–5–10
Total points (maximum possible: 100)	

Collective Efficacy in a PLC at Work® © 2021 Solution Tree Press

SolutionTree.com • Visit **go.SolutionTree.com/PLCbooks** to download this free reproducible.

Driving Force Analysis Process

Purpose Question to Improve	
Driving Forces (+) What's working in the team's favor?	Restraining Forces (−) What's working against your teams?
Actions to reduce the restraining forces: Take one restraining force and identify two actions that will change it to a driving force. 1. 2.	

Source: Adapted from Institute for Healthcare Improvement. (n.d.). Force field analysis [Video file]. Accessed at www.ihi.org/education/IHIOpenSchool/resources/Pages/AudioandVideo/Whiteboard19.aspx on October 2, 2020.

Collective Efficacy in a PLC at Work® © 2021 Solution Tree Press

SolutionTree.com • Visit **go.SolutionTree.com/PLCbooks** to download this free reproducible.

Team Improvement Assessment Questionnaire

For each of the following statements, 1: Not Yet, 2: Partial, 3: Yes.

Date of assessment _____

1. The team is clear on its purpose.   _____

2. The team has explicit ground rules.   _____

3. Members share leadership.   _____

4. The team works to encourage and balance participation of all.   _____

5. The team values, encourages, and effectively manages conflict.   _____

6. The team collaborates rather than competes.   _____

7. Members actively listen to each other.   _____

8. The team works together to make decisions.   _____

9. Team members communicate openly.   _____

10. Members are clear on their roles and assignments.   _____

11. Members recognize and value differences.   _____

12. The team evaluates its own processes to improve them.   _____

13. The team views mistakes as learning opportunities.   _____

14. The team views its work in the context of the system strategic goals.   _____

15. Members encourage and support each other's learning.   _____

Collective Efficacy in a PLC at Work® © 2021 Solution Tree Press

SolutionTree.com • Visit **go.SolutionTree.com/PLCbooks** to download this free reproducible.

BUILDING VISION TO ENHANCE COLLECTIVE EFFICACY

*"Leaders need to be
what they want to see."*

—John C. Maxwell

Let's outline Bandura's definition of collective efficacy one more time: "A group's shared belief in its conjoint capability to organize and execute the courses of action required to produce given levels of attainment" (Bandura, 1997, p. 477). *Execute* is the key word in the context of this chapter.

In *The Four Disciplines of Execution*, Chris McChesney, Sean Covey, and Jim Huling (2012) highlight what they deem the real challenge with execution. McChesney et al. (2012) state:

> Whether you call it a strategy, a goal, or simply an improvement of effort, any initiative you as a leader drive in order to significantly move your team forward will fall into two categories: The first requires mainly a stroke of the pen; the second requires behavioral change. (p. 3)

This awareness encapsulates the dichotomy of execution within the context of vision.

In this chapter, we present how Sanger Unified, using the PLC process, transformed its vision from one educational framework to the next, in a way that continued to build collective efficacy. This experience occurred between 2013 and 2015 and resulted in a vision that honored the past and embraced the new.

The Challenge: Transforming Vision Through Transferrable Principles

Between 2006 and 2012, Sanger's district and school cultures were continuing to evolve while the chemistry and coherence (depth of understanding) of PLCs became clearly evident in the processes and practices that improved student outcomes. A relentless focus on instructional expectations and the integrity (trust) of PLCs served as anchors that grounded the everyday actions of teachers and leaders. Student learning was the unequivocal priority and the primary source for motivating teams of practitioners. Professional relationships trumped personal relationships, and alignment of systems was at its peak. The collective identity of the district had become one of solidarity, deeply rooted in culture and purpose.

Sanger Unified had built a dynamic system that included multiple combinations of shared leadership, reciprocal accountability, and capacity building. This systematic approach ensured cycles of continuous improvement and sustainability across the organization. In *Motion Leadership in Action: More Skinny on Becoming Change Savvy*, Fullan (2013) summarizes key findings by a professional entity specifically analyzing the scope and systematic processes within Sanger Unified. According to Fullan (2013), external evaluators concluded that Sanger had embedded simple systematic processes that enhanced the efficiency of the organization (p. 92). The assessors conclude that Sanger practiced the following.

- Soliciting feedback formally and informally

- Creating multiple intersecting collaborative teams

- Monitoring data frequently

- Constantly adjusting what is tight (namely, rules which all staff members must abide by; DuFour et al., 2016) and loose (namely, elements that are up to the individual educators; DuFour et al., 2016) in response to feedback

The key findings were a reflection of the collaborative work of the district. The summary of findings was grounded in key principles that essentially aligned with Fullan's (2013) change leaders' stances—*change, implementation*, and *sustainability*—as well as many of the sixteen elements that composed them.

Marc Johnson, former Sanger Unified superintendent (2000–2013), highlighted the principles that glued the organization together over time. Leaders translated these principles in a way that was anchored in the PLC process.

- Think big. Envision a dynamic organization with shared responsibility.

- Adhere to a set of core principles and beliefs, and communicate them consistently and clearly in multiple ways, from stories to slogans, and over and over.

- Focus on building the capacity of the system to learn at all levels.

- Foster collaboration up, down, and across the system as a vehicle for continuous learning and shared accountability.

- Focus on a very small number of initiatives that clearly support one another and that can both build on and help develop shared conceptions about what it takes to improve learning.

- Balance demands on educators with the supports they need in order to do what they are being asked to do (Fullan, 2013).

These principles were proven, powerful antecedents of change, implementation, and sustainability. The level of ownership and connectedness to the steadfast vision for over a decade had produced a coalition of practitioners with a laser-like focus on student achievement and results. The district's simple yet comprehensive framework led to high-functioning and efficient actions that boosted organizational confidence and the longevity in continuous improvement. The district's success in raising student achievement and closing the achievement gap had attracted inquiry from school districts across the nation and researchers who sought solutions to the complex challenges of school change. To cast an even brighter spotlight on the organizational success, Marc Johnson was awarded the National Superintendent of the Year award by the American Association of School Administrators in 2011, before retiring in 2013.

However, Sanger's progress was about to be tested, in what Fullan (2013) calls *change savvy*. The test would come in the form of the Common Core State Standards (CCSS). The onset of the CCSS, an educational initiative that details what K–12 students throughout the United States should know by the conclusion of each school grade in English language arts and mathematics, became the next significant challenge for the district.

The Common Core State Standards were adopted by forty-one of the fifty U.S. states, including the state of California, in 2010. In spite of mounting pressure to adopt the standards, including through offers of government grants to states if standards were adopted by August 2010, the district made the decision to intentionally delay the adoption of the CCSS until 2013, providing a buffer to reassess and reevaluate the new vision moving forward that the district would require for the uncharted educational territory ahead. Sanger had spent the previous decade formulating and chiseling out winning strategies for student success. However, the *learning game* had suddenly changed, and educators everywhere were seeking to fully understand the new guidelines, policies, and expectations.

As Fullan (2013) states, "After a comprehensive analysis of CCSS, the district made the decision to become part of California Office to Reform Education (CORE), a collaborative of nine districts that represented almost a quarter of the student population of the state of California. The CORE collaborative grew out of a failed attempt to apply for the federal Race to the Top program" (p. 94). Out of necessity, and in the face of new circumstances and conditions, the demand for a new vision was spotlighted.

The Change

Inspired by the PLC process, Sanger identified three large-scale specific challenges moving forward in regard to its vision. These challenges included:

- *Designing and developing* a new vision under new conditions with all stakeholders

- *Implementing* the new vision, including identifying new capacities and skills and adopting an intentional *learning by doing* approach for implementers and practitioners to propel the organization forward (DuFour et al., 2006, 2010)

- Ensuring organizational structures and systems supported the *execution* of strategies and actions necessary for continuous improvement in light of the organization's vision

Design and Development of the Vision

Designing and developing a new vision would require diligent efforts on behalf of leaders at all levels. Perspectives from many members from all walks of the organization were included in the vision design, including certificated, classified, and community representatives. For example, parents and custodians, who previously had not been considered or included in the district vision design, were now among the architects. After holding several think tanks and receiving collaborative feedback, organizational leaders and stakeholders concluded that the next vision for the district needed to include two dimensions: (1) a compelling dimension that *evokes emotional connection* with meaningful relevancy, and (2) a dimension that gave *accessibility to all*.

A compelling example that evoked emotional connection could be found with Apple Inc. Visionaries such as Steve Jobs, Apple CEO (1996–2011), see the world differently. They foresee grander possibilities than the average person, and they do so with such clarity and precision that they capture the imagination of the masses. They bridge the impossible by making it practical and accessible. District stakeholders wanted to imagine what was possible when powerful student learning was brought to life through relevant application and experiences.

A dimension of the vision that gave *accessibility to all* meant that the language needed to be simple yet profound and needed to give stakeholders the ability to act upon it. A shining example of this can be found in the work of Douglas Reeves, bestselling author of *The Learning Leader: How to Focus School Improvement for Better Results*. According to Reeves (2006), visionary leadership, in the context of education, has dimensions that somewhat contradict the Steve Jobs example. Reeves (2006) asserts that the first obligation of leadership is to articulate a compelling vision, linking clear standards of action that will accomplish the vision. He states, "Visionary leaders are not grandiose, as their visions are more likely to be the blueprint of the architect than the uncertain and cloudy vision of the dreamer. Great visionary leaders challenge the status quo with terminology that is clear and vivid" (Reeves, 2006, p. 35). Reeves (2006) continues, "By definition, vision contemplates the future, and the future inevitably involves uncertainty, change, and fear. Therefore, visions that are fuzzy and described in the haze of mystic reassurance have a counterproductive effect" (p. 35).

Organizational leaders felt it necessary to consider blending these two dimensions of vision to capture the breadth of Sanger's district journey while recognizing the importance of adapting to the change. To begin the process, leaders had to be clear that vision is *not* the following.

- Vision is not an awe-inspiring statement for teams to stand back and stare at on a banner hanging on the wall.
- Vision is not a catchy marketing phrase to promote to the masses.
- Vision is not a glorified fantasy that doesn't relate to the work of all teams.
- Vision should not exist in isolation of organizational goals.
- Vision is not limited to a single speech given at a once-a-year kickoff or welcome-back ceremony.

The district had come to accept that creating a real vision, one that appealed to all members of the district and community, was much greater than what had been achieved so far. The leaders also recognized that if its purpose was to inspire the organization, vision had to be specifically the following.

- Vision must be large enough to capture all other key initiatives of the organization.
- Vision must articulate organizational success and dreams for students.
- Vision must capture our purpose, expectations for our organizational culture, and identity.
- Vision must be simple and yet focused enough for teams to immediately see and experience in their mind's eye what it looks like for them.
- Vision must appeal to all stakeholders: certificated, classified, and community.

Leaders rallied to create a district vision that was crystal clear, where the priority was stated in the context of beliefs. Eventually, in 2013, the leadership defined their work to be meaningful, simple, and compelling enough that the vision could capture all facets of the organization and community. The Sanger Unified vision became the following.

> *We believe* that all students should have options to demonstrate what they learn, and opportunities to be successful and achieve their dreams.

Stakeholders became familiar with two key words: *options* and *opportunities* for children. This combination of a vision aligned with a mission of "increasing student achievement" and a motto of "Every Child, Every Day, Whatever It Takes" formed a new, clearer identity for the organization. This motto was born out of the PLC process and, in turn, has helped shape many foundational PLC resources along the way, including books such as *Every School, Every Team, Every Classroom* by Robert Eaker and Janel Keating (2011). The clarity of purpose meant that the organization's implementation and focus were more about chasing a vision and not about chasing the scoreboard represented by state test scores. The new future was about building success so that all students had meaningful options for learning and opportunities for showcasing their knowledge and skills. This meant that if the organization was fully committed to making the new vision a reality, then student achievement scores would follow as a lag measure of the efforts and actions leading the way.

The *design and development* phase fostered the following outcome: all stakeholders, including community members and classified and certificated staff, as well as partnerships with corporations and universities, could touch and influence the district vision. This was an inspiring revelation for the entire organization.

Implementation of the Vision

There was a distinct recognition by leaders to identify new capacities and skills necessary for continuous improvement while encouraging the *learning-by-doing* approach for implementers and practitioners. Leaders followed this recognition with a sense of urgency to develop an implementation plan that was specific to the actions and practices associated with the new vision, highlighting the options and opportunities for students. Visions, traditionally, are many levels or layers away from the necessary day-to-day actions required to move the current reality of the school or organization forward. It is school leaders who carry the obligation to bridge this divergence, help teams knock the dust off the vision statements, and thrust them into motion. Describing one of the four pillars of a PLC at Work, DuFour et al. (2016) define vision as "What must our school become to accomplish our purpose?" (p. 39). In this context, vision is much more than merely imagining what is possible. It begs the question: What must we do and how must we behave to become the living, breathing version of the vision?

Considering this district practical mindset coupled with the deep-seated beliefs and principles of DuFour et al. (2016), Fullan (2008), Kanold (2011), and DuFour and

Fullan (2013), Sanger made decisions to allocate resources and immediately deploy the following actions.

- School sites developed customized instructional visions that reflected their core values under the guides of district philosophy. Instructional visions ensured action and behavior orientation were connected to expected instructional expectations.

- Monthly district and site professional development opportunities reinforced the alignment of stakeholders to the design and development, implementation, and execution of the new vision.

- District showcases included multiple representatives from each school site, highlighting instructional lessons and student collaborative models that integrated the dimensions of the new vision; allowed for early, middle, and established versions of implementation to be collaboratively shared districtwide over time; and created further outreach among teachers and sites who sought additional learning opportunities to enhance practices with district peers.

- Multilayered coaching and feedback cycles included ongoing classroom observations focused on essential practices that reflected the new vision.

- Data were collected, focusing on elements of the new vision, through observation teams (consisting of rotations of teachers and leaders to determine consistency and quality of implementation throughout the district).

- Technology was integrated across the district (1:1 iPads for all) to ensure access and equity for all students. In addition, technology was viewed as a tool to enhance learning for students, not a simple replacement for paper and pencil.

The *implementation* phase created the following outcomes: (1) all stakeholders sought to impact the new vision through the newly identified capacities and skills, and (2) all stakeholders felt empowered to contribute their expertise while learning from others within and across the system.

Execution of the Vision

To execute the vision, Sanger required a strategy with a synergistic quality that fed the new vision with ongoing supports, feedback, and evaluation. Sanger's leaders identified three essential areas to ensure the prospect of the new vision: (1) investment, (2) alignment, and (3) scalability.

Investment must be strategic. School organizations can have varying decision-making processes in the attempt to develop a compelling vision. District leaders might argue that special time, energy, and processing should be given to the investment of resources. Leaders must strategically focus and allocate resources to directly impact key priorities, such as building individual and collective capacity or instituting improvement cycles focused on the details of implementation. At Sanger, a calculated number of superintendent's designees (at various levels of the organization) was empowered to make decisions in key areas, initiatives, and implementation processes, which provided another opportunity for shared leadership and further ownership of the vision.

Alignment of systems and actions must be recurring and deliberate. Alignment must include a web of collaborative opportunities within and across schools that are data-driven, focused on capacity building, capable of providing ongoing authentic feedback, and encouraging of learning. Let's be clear: alignment doesn't mean matching up diagrams on paper with connecting lines. It includes the deliberate actions of leaders, teachers, and stakeholders at every level. As Collins and Porras (1996) point out in the *Harvard Business Review*, "Building a visionary company requires 99% alignment and 1% vision" (p. 77). District leaders would enthusiastically substantiate this claim.

Scalability must be balanced with fidelity. Small successes by individual teachers and schools create opportunities for shared leadership and reciprocal accountability. Such successes strengthen the systems from the middle of the organization, inherently building confidence, grit, and belief in the practices. These small wins are twofold and reflect the nature of the PLC process. First, the successes help build a guiding coalition of believers, and second, they promote *learning by doing* and refining of practices so that learnings can be shared with other teams' members within and across the system. The ongoing and deliberate processes help shed light on the details and quality of implementation. This spotlight helps teams and leaders measure the level of execution, allowing leaders to gauge the speed of scalability across the systems. This also allows leaders to celebrate and use practitioner growth and progress as exemplars for the entire organization.

Sanger's strategic and systematic supports and action orientation are reflected in the following quote (DuFour et al., 2016):

> A powerful vision results in inspiration, aspiration, and perspiration. It inspires people to rally around a greater purpose. It challenges educators to articulate the school they aspire to create. It leads to action, beginning with building shared knowledge of what it will take to reduce the gap between the vision (what they want to become) and the current reality (who they actually are) of their school and the school-described vision (Williams & Hierck, 2015). (p. 40)

The *execution* phase ensured the following outcomes: (1) Investment in the vision was strategically resourced; financial, social, and professional capital were distributed with a loose–tight framework and adjusted depending on results; (2) vertical and lateral alignment occurred across the entire organization; and (3) massive innovation and scalability were applied to practices and programs.

> ## PRACTITIONER PERSPECTIVE
>
> "In my forty-nine years of experience, I couldn't remember one goal or vision statement. That was, until I created one that had meaning for me. A unifying vision of options and opportunities helped me visualize why my work matters."
>
> **—Albert Mendoza**
> *Custodian,*
> *Sanger Unified School District (1975–2021)*

Leadership Paradoxes

The specific leadership paradoxes Sanger's leadership encountered when building vision to enhance collective efficacy were:

- Clarity vs. focus
- Simplicity vs. complexity

Clarity vs. Focus

Focus and clarity are similar in that they both relate to orienting people or systems toward a target or goal. The difference is that focus, unlike clarity, implies organizational movement toward the vision. Clarity helps eliminate distortions and misconceptions of the vision while focus helps teams gravitate and remain locked into the nuances of the new vision. One of the most critical discoveries for Sanger's leaders was the reality that simply crafting a district vision wasn't enough to create change. Organizational leaders had to wipe the slate clean and restart a process of developing district and site visions that could captivate and connect the work of teams. Leaders needed a vision that provided, as Schmoker (2016) would say, "piercing clarity" (p. 14). To achieve this end, organizational leadership came to the consensus that effective instructional practices were the primary vehicle to increase student academic performance and achievement. If leaders were going to connect all stakeholders to a greater purpose, they would start with creating visions that were meaningful to them—instructional visions.

The challenge sounded simple at first: create a clear instructional vision that connected to the hearts of people and *voilà*, problem solved! What leaders quickly discovered was that just having a well-crafted vision statement wasn't nearly enough to navigate the complexities of the district's transformation needed to meet the CCSS's new demands in teaching and learning. District and site leaders needed to redesign the whole process to be more inclusive and collaborative. Leaders needed to rediscover their *why, what,* and *how* in seeking to meet the demands of the CCSS through the new vision.

Leaders may describe *focus,* on the other hand, as being more closely associated with concentration and continuous, deliberate application. Knowing that the enemy of focus is distraction, leaders were therefore also challenged to eliminate unnecessary distractions for teams.

Increased focus also meant that leaders had to persistently converge collective beliefs and behaviors with structures and processes in an effort to align to the new vision. Leaders would need to move from comprehensive strategic plans to a more refined, simplified message; adopt the "less is more" philosophy; focus on aligned, high-leverage, repeated practices; and work diligently to eliminate programs or initiatives that did not capture the spirit of the new vision.

Simplicity vs. Complexity

Leaders faced the challenge of making the new vision simple enough for all personnel to understand and yet complex enough to honor the dynamics of individuals and teams. The notion of *simplicity* would elicit concern in leaders as some felt the integrity of their visions would be compromised or, in a sense, "dumbed down." Leaders felt that too much simplicity would result in teachers minimizing and short-changing the breadth and depth of best practices. On the other hand, the notion of *complexity* elicited concerns from leaders, as some thought overcomplicating the vision would compromise the clarity and focus of teams. Leaders felt too much complexity would inhibit the actions of teams and potentially paralyze efforts due to confusion, consequently limiting efficiency. Given the volume of learning that needed to take place under the new conditions and climate surrounding the CCSS, balancing simplicity while honoring the complexity of the system would be a formidable challenge for the district.

Leadership Research

The following research helps to complement and build on the paradoxes Sanger's leadership discovered in the challenge. The paradox of discoveries leads us to consider research that either complements or challenges what we learned.

We reviewed research for each of the paradoxes described in the previous section:

- Clarity vs. focus
- Simplicity vs. complexity

Clarity vs. Focus

The Oxford dictionary defines *clarity* as "the quality of being coherent and intelligible; the quality of transparency and purity" (Oxford Lexico, n.d.). Leaders found that clarity must not be a one-time speech or presentation with a constellation of words to navigate. In addition, leaders discovered that clarity of vision must not be implicit; rather, it must be explicit. Clarity of vision means bringing into focus the organization's essentials, the "what we need to become" (DuFour et al., 2010, p. 30), free of distortion or ambiguity. Kanold (2011) supported this claim, asserting:

> Vision should provide a clear and coherent path for future actions. Whether the vision you are casting represents the school or the entire district, the goal is to help people to know, understand, and remember the main idea or the right things to become. (p. 22)

One of Sanger's leadership challenges was the realization that designing a new vision with anything less than "piercing clarity" (Schmoker, 2016, p. 14) may result in a series of consequences detrimental to the organization's ability to actually develop the new vision. Additionally, Schmoker makes the clear case that a lack of clarity has far greater consequences than most leaders realize. According to Schmoker (2016) in his book *Leading With Focus: Elevating the Essentials for School and District Improvement*, leaders should "shun the jargon of academic educationism," which can "wreak havoc on the clear communication that is essential" (pp. 18–19) to improved practice. If leaders wished to craft a powerful vision that resonated with all stakeholders (not the typical educational jargon), then all stakeholders on the front lines would need to have major input in the process of designing a new vision for the future.

In her book *The Outstanding Organization*, author Karen Martin (2012) defines the *focus* of an organization as when leaders dip into and out of projects, mandate the process in progress be replaced with others, redirect resources, overrule decisions, and disappear when leadership support is most needed. Leaders argued that this habitual behavior related to a lack of focus was causing much of the beliefs of the past to constantly surface. What Sanger needed was to focus on a few priorities that were necessary and essential to organization success because this implies consistent movement or progress toward the objective. According to Goleman (2013), leadership hinges on effectively capturing and directing the collective attention: "People make their choices about where to focus based on their perception of what matters to leaders" (p. 211). Attention tends to focus on what has meaning—and what matters. Speaking from a leadership perspective, Goleman (2013) asserts,

> Directing attention toward where it needs to go is primal in leadership. Talent here lies in the ability to shift attention to the right place at the right time, sensing trends and emerging realities and seizing opportunities. But it's not just the focus of one

single strategic decision-maker that makes or breaks a company: it's the entire array of attention bandwidth and dexterity among everyone. (p. 209)

Translation: focus provides the fuel leaders need to bring a synergistic quality to the new vision. It means that all stakeholders—whether they be custodians, bus drivers, librarians, nutritionists, teachers, coaches, or parent volunteers—need to internalize the vision and behave in ways that validate its core message.

Simplicity vs. Complexity

Another dimension of vision that leaders discovered was from the work of Jeffrey Kluger (2008), author of *Simplexity: Why Simple Things Become Complex* (*and How Complex Things Can Be Made Simple*). Kluger (2008) makes the case that "Simplexity" occurs when complex has become simple while the result has dramatically improved—a perfect recipe for powerful change.

Michael Fullan, author of *Motion Leadership: The Skinny on Becoming Change Savvy* (2010), affirms this in regard to the concept of *Simplexity*:

> The skinny is about reducing the weight of the change train. There is too much overload and baggage on the current change journey. The skinny is about Simplexity, finding the smallest number of high-leverage, easy to understand actions that unleash stunningly powerful consequences. It strips away overloaded change—cluttered commotion—and gives us the essential core of what we need in order to get real change owned by the critical mass. (p. 16)

Leaders discovered the undisputed need to inject the concept of Simplexity into the many dimensions of vision. Simplexity essentially armed leaders with the agility to skillfully maneuver situations and conflicts related to the new vision. This maneuverability acted as a sword, cutting through red tape and bureaucracy to the central idea.

REFLECTION QUESTIONS

At this point, stop to consider the paradoxes and research mentioned in the previous sections. Take a moment to answer the following questions to help create further awareness for your own team and organizational collective efficacy.

1. What *conditions* do you need to create to develop a collective vision that communicates behavioral expectations and resonates with all members of the team or organization?

2. What *questions* do you need to ask about your own team's vision that may impact your team or organization?

3. How has your team managed *change* in the face of adversity? What suggestions would you offer to teams after reading this chapter?

Now that you have considered these questions in relation to your own organization, we will share with you the leadership lessons that Sanger learned in their experience of building vision to enhance collective efficacy.

Leadership Lessons on Vision

In this section, we present to the reader our learnings from both the challenge story we experienced at Sanger Unified School District and the research previously presented. We attempt to bring together the challenge, the paradoxes we shared, and what the research asks us to consider in specific examples. The leadership lesson we discuss in this section relates to change-savvy leadership.

In the book *Motion Leadership in Action: More Skinny on Becoming Change Savvy*, Fullan (2013) provides powerful, detailed examples of frameworks, principles, and experiences of school leaders from various parts of the world. These leaders leveraged key drivers within philosophies and formulas to create transformational change within their organizations and beyond. Fullan (2013) found striking commonalities across districts and school institutions that reflected the essential elements of being *change savvy*. Change savvy essentially means that leaders hold true to a small set of core principles that guide their work and navigate the complexities of education accordingly. In our estimation, one of the most applicable essential truths and organizational lessons in *Motion Leadership in Action* is this: *Core principles transfer across visions, contexts, and leaders.*

Sanger's core principles, in short, are as follows: (1) Think big; (2) adhere to core beliefs; (3) build capacity; (4) foster a web of collaboration; (5) focus on a small number of initiatives; and (6) balance demands with supports. These principles are a true reflection of the district's ongoing disciplines that continue to shape the path forward. These principles are deeply rooted and entrenched in the culture of the organization. Even so, when the new challenge of the CCSS revealed itself, it created a tremendous amount of uncertainty and anxiety about the immediate and long-term future of our school communities. The sweeping systematic change across the country tested school districts in a variety of ways and underscored *a leader's* and *leaders'* responsiveness to change. District leaders anchored themselves in a fundamental view that came from Kanold (2011): "A leader in a professional learning community is committed to this adage: 'A shared followership is built not on *who* to follow, but on *what* to follow'" (p. 27). Kanold (2011) furthers this notion, stating, "The voice of the vision and values, not the voice of a single person, must win the day" (p. 27). Stakeholders must understand the vision, reinforce and defend it, teach it, and inspire others to share and own it.

Here's the reality: an organization's vision cannot be lost in a constellation of words, initiatives, or policies. Vision cannot sit passively on shelves or binders, collecting dust. Visions must be alive and in motion.

The depth of understanding and coherence within the Sanger district created a collective grit within and among teams. This resiliency essentially immunized the organization from succumbing to the mounting pressures to conform to an undefined future. The organization's decade-long, ongoing commitment to *learning by doing* had fostered a culture of interdependence rooted in core beliefs that made being *change savvy* powerfully relevant.

Conclusion: Connecting Vision to Collective Efficacy

Execution requires decision makers to strategically allocate resources (of all forms) to implementers and practitioners that have a direct impact on the vision, and to ensure the most essential high-leverage practices (HLPs) are implemented with fidelity to generate results. Sanger's unique combination of a spirited *learning by doing* orientation and a high degree of execution proved meaningful for its leaders in building collective efficacy. In essence, the ability to successfully execute the details of the district's plan through high-leverage actions fortifies the individual and collective beliefs of teams and reinforces the organizational vision.

For leaders to successfully mobilize collaborative teams toward an organizational vision, they must display thoughtful consideration on several fronts. Leaders must empower collaborative teams to *focus* on the details of their actions while providing precision and *clarity* around instructional, assessment, and collaborative expectations. Leaders must assess their current reality and ensure that investments are strategic, alignment of systems and actions are recurring and deliberate, and scalability is balanced with fidelity.

Next Steps

In this section, we provide the reader some simple next steps for teams, associated with the learnings from the text.

- Use the reproducible "1–5–10 Assessment Tool: Vision" (page 68) to assess vision, collaboration, and leadership within your school or organization.

- Use the "Rethinking Organizational Vision, Mission, and Values Graphic Organizer" reproducible on page 69 to realign your school or organization's vision, mission, values, and goals.

1–5–10 Assessment Tool: Vision

Assess and score each of the ten statements, with 1 being the lowest and 10 being the highest. Then calculate your total score.

Overview: Vision	Score
The vision provides a "true north" for all members of the team or organization.	1–5–10
The vision is compelling, laced with an instructional focus where student learning and achievement are the highest priorities.	1–5–10
The vision is manifested in the behaviors of all members of the team or organization.	1–5–10
The vision clearly illustrates what all members of the team or organization must become to accomplish the fundamental purpose.	1–5–10
Collaboration	
The vision is crafted with representation from all members of the team or organization.	1–5–10
The vision honors the voices of all members of the team or organization.	1–5–10
Leadership	
Leaders reflect the spirit of the vision by intentionally engaging all members of the team or organization emotionally.	1–5–10
Leaders reflect the spirit of the vision by intentionally engaging all members of the team or organization intellectually.	1–5–10
Leaders reflect the spirit of the vision by deeply connecting to the aspirations of all members of the team or organization.	1–5–10
Leaders reflect the spirit of the vision by creating conditions of celebration, including expressions of appreciation and admiration.	1–5–10
Total points (maximum possible: 100)	

Collective Efficacy in a PLC at Work® © 2021 Solution Tree Press

SolutionTree.com • Visit **go.SolutionTree.com/PLCbooks** to download this free reproducible.

Rethinking Organizational Vision, Mission, and Values Graphic Organizer

Sample XYZ Unified: Rethinking vision, mission, and values for building collective team efficacy

Vision/Mission/Values	What is our Vision?	What is our Mission?	What are our Values/Principles?
	To have all students meet, exceed, excel, and contribute in society	To improve student achievement	Never give up. All students can succeed.

What are the goals of the team/organization? (Define at least three.)

Build a foundation and culture of a PLC.

Create a multitiered system of supports so all students can succeed.

Use high-quality instructional practices in all classrooms that engage all students.

How?

Leadership: How does leadership reflect the spirit of our vision? What do we do and say that align our mission and vision?

Collaboration: How do we honor voices in our vision and mission? How do we revisit our vision and mission on a regular basis?

If we make sure that everything we do is focused on supporting the vision and mission of our team, then what will we be able to do?

Collective Efficacy in a PLC at Work® © 2021 Solution Tree Press

SolutionTree.com • Visit **go.SolutionTree.com/PLCbooks** to download this free reproducible.

BUILDING BELIEF AND ACCOUNTABILITY TO ENHANCE COLLECTIVE EFFICACY

"Beliefs are deeply embedded in a cultural tapestry, and they shape thoughts and actions in powerful ways."

—Terrence E. Deal and Kent D. Peterson

According to Caproni (2017), beliefs predict our motivation, persistence, and engagement as we pursue goals. Beliefs determine our levels of resiliency when faced with obstacles and whether we approach challenges with confidence. Thus, beliefs make up an essential component in the building of collective efficacy. Additionally, accountability is the mechanism that ensures that the beliefs of teams align with behaviors. With internal, reciprocal accountability, change happens. Without it, processes break down very quickly. According to Connors & Smith (2011), within an accountability culture, "people at every level of the organization embrace their role in facilitating the change and demonstrate the ownership needed for making true progress, both for themselves and their organization" (p. 1). Accountability is what allows teams to acknowledge and validate members (creating small wins), which builds confidence and perseverance attributes that foster collective efficacy. By combining fierce belief and reciprocal accountability, leaders can accelerate change, leading to enhanced collective efficacy within and across the school organization.

In this chapter, we share what the organization learned from our experiences with Fairmont Elementary (2000–2017). Specifically, the chapter targets how leaders can enhance collective teacher efficacy when teams cultivate a collaborative culture in which belief systems and internal accountability reinforce the strategic alignment to the organizational vision. Fairmont's fierce beliefs and shared accountability increased with an underlying emphasis on clarity of teacher expectations, greater interdependence among teams, and a challenge mindset that pushed the customary boundaries within instruction, assessment, and collaboration.

This convergence of beliefs and accountability invigorated the school, empowering teacher and student teams through innovative, strategic processes such as Fairmont's Special Teams (STs) and Student Learning Communities (SLCs), described later in the "Leadership Lessons" section of this chapter (page 83). Fairmont's blend of deep conviction to systematic improvement and accountability through interdependence spawned an extremely high, almost tangible, degree of collective teacher efficacy.

The Challenge: The Fairmont Story

Fairmont Elementary is a TK–8 (transitional kindergarten to eighth grade) school with a unique personality, pride, and identity. With a tradition of long-time staffers and a supportive, inclusive community, Fairmont's encouraging, inviting, and close-knit atmosphere had always attracted families from across the district to this school. It was not uncommon for three generations of families to have attended Fairmont, dating back to the early 1900s. However, by the early 2000s, with the onset of No Child Left Behind (NCLB) and its significant consequences for schools that did not close student achievement gaps, Fairmont's story began to drastically shift. Student achievement had recently stagnated, and the unrelenting challenge of raising student achievement scores while closing the achievement gap had created organizational tension, along with a clear opportunity for change.

The challenges embedded within Fairmont's story were *not* born of team dysfunction—quite the opposite. It was a traditional school made up of amazing individuals with tremendous pride who worked well together. Fairmont's test would come in the form of a collective decision: would the school be willing to do *whatever it takes* to move from a good school to a *great* school? This crossroads led to the following predicaments.

- Staff willingness (or unwillingness) to change
- Competition from a neighboring district
- Rising demands
- Families seeking higher academic standards

The effects of NCLB were testing staff willingness to evolve and change in what was becoming a less consistent and predictable school environment. Fairmont was becoming more diversified in terms of student demographics. Achievement gaps in various areas were more prominent, and the reasons for these gaps were multidimensional. Further, a growing English learner population had highlighted the need to integrate and differentiate instruction to meet the needs of all learners.

Fairmont shared a border with another high-performing, well-known school district that had built a new, state-of-the-art high school. This created a glaring issue because some families were leaving Fairmont and Sanger for what they perceived as better educational and co-curricular options in the neighboring district, and that would mean a major loss in school and district enrollment-based funding.

Multigenerational families, as well as new families coming into Fairmont, expected the school to meet the rising demands of expectations and performance and offer career and technical enrichment options and opportunities for students while also meeting the greater needs of a more diverse student population who required more resources, intensive supports, and interventions. (As a specific example, the number of identified special education and English learners had grown by almost 20 percent over the three previous years.) The pressures of meeting the demands of NCLB, including state test scores and closing the achievement gap, accentuated ongoing and growing community complaints to the district office, resulting in friction between the district leadership and school staff regarding vision alignment.

In 2000, Sanger Unified had formed a K–8 environmental charter school less than four miles from Fairmont, producing yet another layer of complexity. This newly established charter school had an innovative concept that further distinguished it from other schools, specifically Fairmont. The new charter school attracted and captured students and families who were seeking the highest academic standards that Fairmont appeared to be missing; however, there was a dismissive tone by a few staffers regarding the growing number of students and families leaving. This gave district leadership pause as to the level of ownership by team members. Other staffers were internally rationalizing that charters are different than public schools; therefore, expectations for innovation at Fairmont were somewhat tempered by public school constraints. The challenge then was creating a heightened sense of urgency and belief that Fairmont's joint efforts and commitment to interdependence could help transform the Sanger Unified PLC from *good* to *great*.

The Change

During this challenging time, a new principal, Jared Savage, had been hired for the school. At the onset of being hired, Savage sought to assess the efficiency and effectiveness of collaborative teams while instituting a philosophy that empowered students as owners of their learning. Savage brought high-energy engagement, renewed expectations, and a focus on reciprocal accountability and shared leadership.

Savage was known for his passionate coaching approach to leadership and was both unafraid and unapologetic about challenging the norm. In addition, the high degree of conviction to a new path made for a captivating spirit and raised the expectations for teams, requiring full commitment to the following.

- Individual and collective accountability to the Sanger Unified vision through interdependence

- Openness to challenging one's belief systems through engaging conversations and action alignment

- Openness to challenging one's behaviors and habits that were misaligned with the Sanger Unified vision

- Willingness to engage students as learning partners with embedded opportunities for voice and choice

As the staff beliefs and expectations intensified, *most* of the staff grew in affirmation and acceptance. We say *most* because Mr. Savage had built a guiding coalition of believers, strong enough to send a clear, powerful message to those who initially resisted change: you are either fully committed to the vision, process, and change mindset, or you are not. And if you are not, your unwillingness or indifference will be challenged at every turn.

Other Sanger school leaders became increasingly intrigued specifically by what was happening at Fairmont. Various instructional observations by Sanger leadership provided qualitative evidence that teams at Fairmont were explicitly held accountable for moving away from silos (team members operating in isolation) to teaming structures precisely designed to empower shared leadership, shared accountability, and shared beliefs to improve student outcomes.

A stark transformation quickly ensued, and staff's clarity of expectations began to develop the following three constructs: (1) instructional expectations, (2) quality formative assessments, and (3) improving the collaborative practices of teams. Fairmont's collaborative teams were focused on conversations about student data and results-oriented formative assessments. Interdependence was not optional—teams had to learn together, share together, and focus together. Shared leadership was an expectation of all staff and intentionally embedded into all functions of the school.

Previous mindsets of working together in teams would sometimes manifest in the following staff actions or beliefs:

- Moderate compliance with expectations, by self or peers, was acceptable.

- Assessment of student learning data in collaborative team meetings was inconsistent.

- Independence, instead of interdependence, was not directly confronted.

- Team discussions and planning could be derailed or hindered by individual resisters.

With a newly inspired belief system and an expectation of internal accountability, Fairmont moved to solidify and bolster the already established PLC model demonstrated by the following behaviors:

- Mutual accountability by *all* staff to established collective commitments
- Deep commitment by *all* to beliefs and behaviors aligned with a new vision
- Embedded data-driven, results-oriented practices and protocols in *all* collaborative teams
- Shared leadership, including the expectation that *all* will contribute to collaborative efforts and strategies for improvement
- Multilayered feedback cycles for *all* in the areas of instruction, assessment, and collaboration

The nuance from previous behaviors was that both leadership accountability and reciprocal accountability within collaborative teams were collectively shared and owned. The critical learning in the Fairmont story is that site leadership held and elicited strong beliefs and accountability, specifically for collaboration and instructional expectations. The focus and clarity elevated the site's ability to align with the district's vision for collaborative teams, building new behaviors that enhanced their school practices and performance. Fierce beliefs reinforced mutual accountability measures, and the mutual accountability measures reinforced the fierce beliefs. State test scores drastically improved over consecutive years; achievement gaps were significantly closed; transfers from Fairmont to the northern district, as well as the charter school to the east, essentially halted; and families that originally left Fairmont began to return with a restored confidence and outlook for what was not only possible, but more importantly, what they expected.

PRACTITIONER PERSPECTIVE

"The Fairmont team has built a culture of unrelenting improvement and a fierce belief in their collective ability to impact student lives."

—Tim Lopez
Associate Superintendent of Curriculum and Instruction,
Sanger Unified

Leadership Paradoxes

The specific leadership paradoxes Sanger's leadership encountered when building belief and accountability to enhance collective efficacy were:

- Beliefs vs. behaviors

- Teacher empowerment vs. student empowerment

- Innovation vs. cultivation

Beliefs vs. Behaviors

One of the first paradoxes that we needed to explore was understanding how to balance beliefs and behaviors to generate collective team efficacy—an interesting dynamic that becomes a significant part of the Fairmont story.

Belief may be defined as trust, faith, or confidence in someone or something. Beliefs in schools are typically expressed in phrases such as "do what is best for kids" or "whatever it takes." Beliefs may be deeply rooted in religion or moral purpose, and even linked to specific situations or contexts. Beliefs not only impact a person's perceptions—how they think, what they think, and the lens through which they view the world—they also directly and indirectly influence behaviors as well.

Behavior, on the other hand, may be defined as the way in which one conducts oneself, especially toward others. Behaviors, just like beliefs, can be deep-seated, with various historical perspectives and interpretations of events, habits, and motivations. Behaviors are expressed in actions that, if continued over time, become habits that can be very beneficial or extremely detrimental to the organization. Leaders must recognize that behaviors emerge from multiple sources, such as intrinsic or extrinsic motivational factors. Behaviors (positive or negative) consequently shape the perceptions, opinions, and beliefs of other team members.

Typically, in schools, we see leaders assume that changes in behavior occur only after beliefs (or mindsets) change within the individual or teams. However, we would challenge this assumption and ask leaders to consider the possibility that behaviors must change first, and that, with some measure of success, changes in beliefs will follow suit.

The reciprocal relationship between beliefs and behaviors becomes an interesting dynamic for district leaders to consider. Leaders must determine the best course of action to balance the coordination between beliefs and behaviors. Questions to consider in this context may be:

- Should leaders focus primarily on beliefs to enhance collective efficacy?

- Should leaders focus primarily on behaviors to enhance collective efficacy?

- Should leaders target both beliefs and behaviors simultaneously to impact collective efficacy?

The paradox presented an interesting dilemma: changing beliefs may not exist in a vacuum. Leaders need to carefully consider that it may be a change in behaviors (through experiential success) that actually elicits a change in beliefs.

Teacher Empowerment vs. Student Empowerment

Considering how to build both teacher and student empowerment created another interesting paradox at Fairmont. Traditionally, school organizations seek to empower teachers by increasing capacity and opportunities through various leadership roles. In turn, by embracing a philosophy of empowering adults, organizations believe the end result will be positive achievement outcomes for students. It goes without saying that empowering teachers, especially in the areas of instruction, assessment, and collaboration, is instrumental in strengthening the effectiveness of teaching practices and building collective efficacy. Ultimately, schools that create ample shared leadership opportunities for teachers serve as powerful antecedents of change.

However, limiting empowerment to solely teachers within the school system can be a monumental mistake by leaders. Although collective teacher efficacy constructs are powerful in a myriad of ways, leaders may consider building *student* efficacy as a source for improvement—a potential game changer for schools. The reality is that there is a treasure trove of simmering potential that lies within students and remains untapped in education. What's missing, in our assessment of the education system as a whole, is *how* students should be or could be involved in the learning process beyond basic engagement practices in the classroom. This led Sanger's leadership to consider a drastically different model—one that treated students as learning partners. The possibilities for more meaningful student ownership and deeper learning in the classroom became the new philosophy. Fairmont's SLCs concept (discussed in "Leadership Lessons on Belief and Accountability," page 83) created an exciting new approach to further engage students in the learning process.

Innovation vs. Cultivation

Schools in every district often face an assortment of initiatives that challenge leaders to find the equilibrium between chasing new, innovative, and promising practices versus cultivating and nurturing more of what already works. *Innovation* can be described as a new method, idea, or product. *Cultivation* can be defined as the process of trying to develop a quality or skill that already exists. Leaders sometimes experience the angst of weighing the decision to support teams in ways that allow for innovation and creative processes to occur versus the fear of being viewed by senior district leadership as a nonconformer to district processes and protocols. Within every initiative, philosophy, approach, or strategy, there should be room for autonomy and innovation. The loose-tight approach (Kanold, 2011) had to be weighed by site leadership. Kanold (2011) asserts,

> In professional learning community leadership, you get "tight" about the "right thing" components of your shared vision, and then you turn that vision into action by being "loose" with how the vision is accomplished by those responsible for implementation. (p. 42)

This type of approach may run the risk of staff perceiving leaders as steering teacher practices away from prioritized district initiatives, even though this may not be the reality. Leaders also face the oxymoron of honoring existing school or district systems through cultivation, while walking the line of innovations within the guidelines set by district philosophy. Fairmont had certainly found traction to systematically foster innovative teaching ideas while simultaneously cultivating a deep collaborative spirit focused on being champions for student learning.

Leadership Research

The following research helps to complement and build on the paradoxes Sanger's leadership discovered in the challenge. The paradox of discoveries leads us to consider research that either complements or challenges what we learned.

We reviewed research for each of the paradoxes described in the previous section:

- Beliefs vs. behaviors

- Teacher empowerment vs. student empowerment

- Innovation vs. cultivation

Beliefs vs. Behaviors

Fairmont's story brought to light the belief vs. behavior dynamic that researchers and experts have highlighted in multiple ways. In her book, *The Science of Success: What Researchers Know That You Should Know,* Paula Caproni (2017) discusses the science of beliefs in a powerful way.

> After decades of studying how our beliefs affect us, researchers have found that our beliefs about ourselves, others, and how the world works predict how high we set our goals and whether we succeed in achieving them. Our beliefs predict our motivation, persistence, and engagement as we pursue our goals, as well as our resilience when faced with setbacks. Our beliefs predict whether we seek out hard problems or take the easy way out, whether we take risks or play it safe, whether we admit mistakes or hide them (or blame others), whether we seek out negative as well as positive feedback, whether we ask for help or go it alone, whether we take time to coach others or expect them to fend for themselves, whether we handle transitions well or crumble, and whether we remain strong when faced with prejudice or internalize unfair stereotypes. (p. 27)

The fundamental point in Caproni's (2017) message is that beliefs are powerful predictors of outcomes and essentially influence how individuals react and respond to all contexts, circumstances, and challenges. As Caproni (2017) states, "Beliefs rest on faith rather than evidence" (p. 66). Beliefs are powerful in schools, especially in the case of Fairmont, because they reflect the core values regarding student and teacher capacity, while bridging the divide between teaching and learning.

Similar to beliefs, experts and researchers would also argue that behaviors can be considered a powerful (if not the primary) source for change within schools. In 2004, Richard Elmore published *School Reform from the Inside Out: Policy, Practice, and Performance*. In it, Elmore (2004) asserts that the principal challenge and foremost problem of any change initiative is "changing people's behavior" (p. 2).

Additionally, DuFour and DuFour (2012), in their book *The School Leader's Guide to Professional Learning Communities at Work*, note that in an effort to shift behaviors, school leaders should consider two critical levers to elicit behavioral change.

> The most powerful lever for changing professional practice is concrete evidence of irrefutable results. A second powerful lever for changing behavior and professional practices is the positive peer pressure that comes along with being a member of a team that is working interdependently to achieve a common goal for which members are mutually accountable. (p. 56)

Fairmont was exceptional in utilizing these types of levers to encourage positive behavioral changes and promote the conditions necessary for enhanced beliefs and collective efficacy.

School leaders must carefully weigh the conundrum of balancing beliefs and behaviors. Considering the research and a need for deeper understanding, most leaders would argue that full alignment of beliefs and behaviors can serve as powerful antecedents of change. A key priority for leaders, then, is to confront the discrepancies in beliefs and behaviors of individuals and teams so that healthy dialogue and deeper understanding can occur. When schools like Fairmont are able to put processes in place to align and reinforce beliefs and behaviors, the foundation is set to drastically boost collective efficacy.

Teacher Empowerment vs. Student Empowerment

Teacher empowerment is a longstanding vital construct within schools and will continue to be as the education system evolves. Bill Gates, cofounder of the technology giant Microsoft, is quoted as saying, "As we look ahead into the next century, leaders will be those who empower others" (Strategies for Influence, n.d.). In turn, putting Gates's lens on the educational system, school leaders who empower others inherently give teachers and teacher teams a "license to lead."

Considering Gates's thoughts, empowerment is key to organizational transformation and can have major implications for enhanced collective efficacy. First and foremost, it is imperative to understand that the empowerment of teacher leaders and collective efficacy are inherently connected. Second, it is important to note that while the *why* (the purpose) of teacher empowerment is hardly disputable, the *how* (the implementation) of teacher empowerment is more challenging. According to Lai and Cheung (2015), teacher leaders, self-efficacy, and collective teacher efficacy are all interconnected. Furthermore, Lai and Cheung (2015) identify four different types of teacher leadership to consider when empowering teachers to take on roles within the organization. Teacher leadership roles may:

- Be individually or collectively based
- Be transformational in nature
- Function within communities of practice
- Support school development at different levels

Jenni Donohoo and Moses Velasco (2016) reinforce this notion of empowering teachers, emphasizing that within shared leadership, leaders should resist the temptation to individually solve problems but rather invest the time needed for others to discover what works best. They state, "When formal leaders provide opportunities for shared leadership by affording others the power to make decisions, everyone benefits" (Donohoo & Velasco, 2016, p. 21). In this shared leadership model, decision making is turned over to the teachers, and leaders actively seek opinions to produce solutions. Therefore, leaders must build and embolden the organization by increasing the volume of opportunities for teacher voices to advance the collective capacity and efficacy of teams, as in the case of Fairmont.

In stark contrast to teacher empowerment, student empowerment has *not* been a longstanding construct that the education system has strategically employed to enhance academic achievement, even though most educators would argue it is an essential part of the solution. Student empowerment has often been limited to lip service, and most leaders would contend that the idealistic theories are a far cry from daily classroom practices across schools and districts, even though years of research adamantly advocate for increases in strategies and supports to boost student ownership in the learning process. John Hattie (2009) references the aspect of *visible learning*, which he defines as "when teachers see learning through the eyes of the students and when students see themselves as their own teachers" (p. 238). Hattie (2009) adds to this notion, proclaiming that teachers should "work as a coach, not a scorekeeper" in order to enhance the learning environment for students (p. 240). By engaging and empowering students to be partners in their learning, leaders create instantaneous ownership, invaluable student voice and agency, and accentuated opportunities for student growth.

Another example of research that supports student ownership of their learning comes from Kim Bailey and Chris Jakicic (2012). In *Common Formative Assessment: A Toolkit for Professional Learning Communities at Work*, Bailey and Jakicic (2012) include an entire chapter devoted to engaging students as "partners in the learning process" (p. 84). Furthermore, students must be emboldened to be in control and empowered to change the course of their learning—in other words, they become more responsible and able to respond. Students are no longer being "done to" by the teacher; they are actually working in partnership with the teacher to learn at higher levels. (Bailey & Jakicic, 2012, p. 84)

Bailey and Jakicic (2012) note key ingredients to student empowerment and ownership of learning, all of which apply to Fairmont's SLCs. These include engaging students in defining quality work, providing feedback that is geared toward self-reporting (not grades), and establishing partnerships with students to monitor progress by identifying strengths and weaknesses in the learning process.

Innovation vs. Cultivation

There are several sources of research and expertise that endorse the need to balance innovation and cultivation within school organizations. For starters, leaders who are *innovators* are powerful change agents within organizations. In his book *The Innovator's Mindset: Empower Learning, Unleash Talent, and Lead a Culture of Creativity*, George Couros (2015) writes, "innovation is not about the stuff; it is a way of thinking" (p. 35). Couros (2015) makes the claim that leaders with an Innovator's Mindset have a "belief that abilities, intelligence, and talents are developed so that they lead to the creation of new and better ideas" (p. 34). This constant focus on bettering the systems, processes, or efficiency of the organization is critical to prevent inertia and stagnation. Innovation requires reimagination. Couros (2015) reinforces this notion, asserting "Savvy leaders understand the need for innovation and, as a result, constantly reinvent their organization" (p. 18).

In order for teams to embrace the Innovator's Mindset, beliefs must be held in alignment with the spirit of ongoing improvement and efficiency. In order for innovation to enrich schools, teachers must have the freedom to consider ideas and test improvement practices in a nonthreatening environment. It is foundational for innovative school cultures to be fortified in an unwavering *belief* and *trust* in the collaborative relationships between teachers and leaders.

Although innovation typically attracts the most recognition and accolades for teams, leaders might consider that *cultivation* continues to be the unsung hero in education. Leaders with the ability to nourish culture and build upon the individual and collective strengths of teams have a much greater chance to enhance positive beliefs and collective efficacy within schools. Cultivation theoretically prepares the school's soil for academic performance growth opportunities. In *Coherence: The Right Drivers in Action for Schools, Districts, and Systems*, Fullan and Quinn (2016) emphasize the importance of cultivation in school cultures: "We need leaders who create a culture of growth; know how to engage the hearts and minds of everyone; and focus their collective intelligence, talent, and commitment to shaping a new path" (p. 47). Fullan and Quinn (2016) emphasize four key areas that, if mastered by leaders, can be "leveraged within and across organizations and build coherence for impact" (p. 48). The four areas include:

1. A culture of growth (learning, innovation, and action)

2. Learning leadership "lead learners" (principals that indirectly and explicitly influence the group)

3. Capacity building (development of knowledge, skills, and commitments)

4. Collaborative work (a meaningful degree of collaborative practices toward sustained behavior)

Cultivation in this context refers to not only the refinement of practices and deeper collaborative learning, but a culture that embraces the spirit of nurturing the people and processes within it. Therefore, school leaders must carefully consider how to balance the nuances of innovation and cultivation when attempting to enhance collective teacher efficacy.

REFLECTION QUESTIONS

At this point, stop to consider the paradoxes and research mentioned in the previous sections. Take a moment to answer the following questions to help create further awareness for your own team and organizational collective efficacy.

• Does your school or team intentionally make efforts to build alignment of beliefs and behaviors that reflect the organizational vision?

• Does your school or team confront discrepancies or misalignment between beliefs and behaviors of team members? Why or why not?

• Does your school or team create and promote processes that empower teachers and students? Why or why not?

- Does your school or team capture a balance between cultivating best practices while creating a nonthreatening environment where innovative thought can be considered and tested?

What do mutual accountability and shared leadership look like within your site or organization? What might be some considerations for improvement in these areas? Now that you have considered these questions in relation to your own organization, we will share with you the leadership lessons that Sanger learned in their experience of building belief and accountability to enhance collective efficacy.

Leadership Lessons on Belief and Accountability

In this section, we present what we have learned from both the site-based challenge experienced at Fairmont and the research previously presented. We attempt to bring together the challenge, the paradoxes we shared, and what the research asks us to consider in specific examples. The leadership lesson we discuss in this section is the power of teams.

The critical learnings from this chapter reinforce the unequivocal power of team interdependence and its impact on collective efficacy. Schools like Fairmont, which have leaders who are deeply committed to building a sense of empowerment for staff and students as well as an unwavering belief in a vision, can truly inspire teams for change. The most meaningful lesson learned from Fairmont's success was the power of teaming structures. Fairmont's teaming structures fostered shared leadership and accountability anchored to a core set of beliefs that provided a crystal-clear identity, a sense of connectedness for all stakeholders, and a relentless commitment to the vision.

Fairmont's leaders strategically created a novel teaming structure called *Special Teams* to empower teacher leaders. Within the Special Teams model, ten focus areas (each one a special team) were created for staff members to voluntarily commit to teams that matched passions to strengths, talents, and expertise. The Special Teams structure galvanizes school staffers through shared leadership—a network of feedback and decision-making processes to create greater impact on performance and efficiency within the school. The ten Special Teams include:

1. Leadership

2. Curriculum and Instruction

3. English Language Development

4. Marketing

5. Organization

6. Agriculture/STEM

7. Social-Emotional Learning

8. Professional Development

9. College and Career

10. Innovation

Special Teams fostered both capacity and coherence within and across teams to problem solve or address particular challenges within the organization.

Fairmont's teachers were also invigorated to bolster a new learning culture highlighting a student empowerment model: Student Learning Communities (SLCs). SLCs operate similarly to teacher collaborative teams: jointly establishing collective commitments; designating roles and responsibilities; setting SMART goals; determining collaborative expectations; and creating multiple learning progressions to measure growth. SLCs are given deep learning opportunities to analyze, critique, and discuss learning results while identifying challenges to close learning gaps. Heightened learning expectations were created through teacher-student co-designed rubrics centered around 21st century learning (the 4 Cs)—*communication, collaboration, critical thinking*, and *creativity*. This framework has in recent years expanded to include two additional Cs—*citizenship* and *character*—following the work of *New Pedagogies for Deep Learning* (Fullan, Quinn, & McEachen, 2018) and ongoing research and development.

Using research such as Bailey and Jakicic (2012), Fullan, Quinn, and McEachen (2018), and Hattie (2009, 2016), Fairmont has sought to legitimize student empowerment in the learning process by creating a framework that included structures, processes, enabling conditions, and student-led learning as cornerstones of the work. Embedded within the SLC framework are growth opportunities for students in the areas of capacity, coherence, and connection (relevancy). This convergence of essential elements within the SLC framework promotes powerful learning partnerships between students, teachers, and leaders.

The SLC framework spawned a culture that essentially brought to life a level of collective team efficacy among students, traditionally absent from education and classrooms. After years of refinement, the excitement and synergy created through teachers' collaborative work in SLCs came to fruition in 2013. In his closing statements to Sanger Unified, Irvin Howard, former president of the National Forum to Accelerate Middle-Grades Reform, stated, "I have been across the United States on school visitations and never heard of or seen Student Learning Communities until I came to Fairmont. Now I believe Student Learning Communities belong in every school across the nation" (I. Howard, personal communication, March 27,

2013). In addition, Sanger Unified School District received the *Golden Bell Award*, given through the California School Boards Association (CSBA), in 2014 for outstanding programs and best practices in the category of *Closing the Achievement Gap*. Specifically, the honor was given to Sanger for the impact of Student Learning Communities, originating at Fairmont, based on student performance outcomes.

Another example and philosophical visual for empowering teams was Fairmont's clear and compelling *creed*—ten core school beliefs that fuel and boost all other facets of the organization. Merriam-Webster's Collegiate Dictionary (2007) defines *creed* as "a set of fundamental beliefs; *also*: a guiding principle" (p. 294). A creed is essentially a set of beliefs, principles, or opinions that strongly influence the way people live or work. From an educational perspective, a creed is a set of collective ideals or operating norms upon which an organization builds its strategic philosophy. Fairmont's creed had massive implications for culture, purpose, and vision attainment. It captured and captivated the collective identity and brand of the school community. Although the creed is unique to Fairmont, the beliefs and principles can transfer to any school organization. Figure 4.1 showcases Fairmont's creed.

The Fairmont Creed

1. 1–0, that's all that matters.
2. We are the hammer and the light.
3. We have simple, effective schemes.
4. We fully understand relationships.
5. We protect the sacred ground.
6. We challenge negative attitudes and behaviors.
7. We own a collective growth mindset.
8. We win in the learning game.
9. We stand for both tradition and innovation.
10. We inspire championship culture!

Figure 4.1: The Fairmont Creed.

The first belief listed on the creed is "1–0, that's all that matters." Using the sports analogy, *1–0*, teams believe that what matters most is winning the day by ensuring high degrees of student learning within an inspiring learning environment. "We are the hammer and the light" means teams believe in breaking barriers that hinder organizational progress while simultaneously serving as a beacon for others to follow. "We have simple, effective schemes" means that teams understand the complexities of the school system but collectively and strategically choose to focus on a few simple strategies with the most impact on student achievement. "We fully understand relationships" means that teams recognize the power of connections through shared leadership and reciprocal accountability. "We protect the sacred ground" translates to Fairmont's commitment to defending the most critical values of the organization, such as the three big ideas of a PLC (DuFour et al., 2016). "We challenge negative attitudes and behaviors" signifies that teams believe in confronting negativity, pessimism, and toxic attitudes and behaviors. "We own a collective growth mindset" means that teams believe that with effort, persistence, and development, collaborative efforts will translate to enhanced teacher efficacy and increased student performance. "We win in the learning game" means that teams believe that education can be viewed as a "learning game." *Winning* translates to growth; ideally, that students show at least one year of academic growth for one year of input (Hattie, 2016). "We stand for both tradition and innovation" signifies that teams believe in the importance of honoring best practices, past or present, that produce positive results while promoting and encouraging teachers to explore and test new ideas that may prove more effective. "We inspire championship culture!" means that teams believe that the purpose of educators is to create deep, meaningful, relevant, and inspirational learning environments for students where they can become champions of their own learning and lives. It's important to note here that school philosophies always fall under the guides of district mission, vision, values, and goals. The school philosophy was a reflection of the personal and collective experiences, directly related to the Fairmont story.

Conclusion: Connecting Belief and Accountability to Collective Efficacy

Ultimately, leaders who demonstrate the combination of strategic practices, incorporation of research, and shared leadership models enhance collective team efficacy by:

- Consistently aligning, realigning, and reinforcing belief constructs and actions through reciprocal accountability

- Empowering both teacher and student teams through shared leadership opportunities

- Displaying deep commitment to a vision and the confidence to execute the actions necessary to move closer to vision attainment

- Building capacity around a collective growth mindset and inherently building resiliency attributes and perseverance to combat challenges and promote positive change

Our unique experience at Fairmont helped inform our leadership learnings. Fierce belief and shared accountability to a compelling vision are essential to building powerful coalitions that promote and foster collective efficacy. Leaders who intentionally cultivate a culture that empowers teacher teams to be valuable contributors to solutions (like Fairmont's Special Teams), and bolster student teams as partners in learning (like Fairmont's SLCs), will inevitably foster high degrees of collective efficacy within teams.

Next Steps

In this section, we provide the reader some simple next steps to take as a team associated with the learnings from the readings.

- Use the reproducible "1–5–10 Assessment Tool: Leadership" shown on page 88 to assess leadership within your school or organization.

- Use the reproducible "Special Teams Starter Template" (page 89) to identify key areas within your team or organization that may benefit from a shared leadership model.

- Use the reproducible "Student Learning Community (SLC) Starter Template" on page 90 to begin considering what student empowerment by design will look like within your team or organization.

1–5–10 Assessment Tool: Leadership

Assess and score each of the ten statements, with 1 being the lowest and 10 being the highest. Then calculate your total score.

Leadership	Score
Leadership creates ongoing clarity around mission, vision, values, and goals.	1–5–10
Leadership creates ongoing opportunities to build competence, capacity, and coherence.	1–5–10
Leadership provides clear expectations for loose–tight processes and systems.	1–5–10
Leadership serves as both *leader* and *learner*.	1–5–10
Leadership actively engages and empowers adults and students in the learning process.	1–5–10
Leadership intentionally contributes to teams by actively engaging in professional development, PLCs, and other activities as a productive team member.	1–5–10
Leadership is sharply focused on priorities and eliminates distractions.	1–5–10
Leadership manages conflict and confrontation with dignity and respectfully challenges negative attitudes and beliefs.	1–5–10
Leadership creates moments to honor and celebrate adult and student progress and performance.	1–5–10
Leadership creates ongoing opportunities for teams to build connection through shared leadership opportunities.	1–5–10
Leadership values testing and reflection of innovative practices that create deeper learning opportunities for students.	1–5–10
Total points (maximum possible: 100)	

Special Teams Starter Template

School Name: _____

Vision for Special Teams: _____

Example Team	Example Focus	Example Specific Task	Example Timeline
Leadership	Establish beliefs and accountability.	Design a fishbowl activity to help teams align beliefs and accountability.	August 2021
Curriculum and Instruction	Evaluate grade-level assessments for quality.	Use the site-based Quality Assessment Tool (QAT) to summarize (one page) schoolwide.	September 2021
English Language Development	Develop goal-setting orientation for teachers and students.	Develop Individualized Language Plans (ILPs) for students.	October 2021
Marketing	Find creative ways to showcase, brand, and promote your school identity.	Design a canvas or digital storyboard (to be displayed in the cafeteria) to tell the school's history. Blend elements of community traditions and new innovations.	August 2021
Organization	Manage curriculum pacing guides, assessments, and SLCs.	Develop a user-friendly digital color-coded pacing guide with links to grade-level assessments.	October 2021
Agriculture/STEM (Your school focus here)	Design schoolwide agriculture/STEM focus in curricula, activities, and project-based learning.	Seamlessly blend and design three sample agriculture and engineering lessons for grades TK–8, with a focus on college and career opportunities.	October 2021
Social-Emotional Learning (SEL)	Utilize SEL resources to increase schoolwide awareness.	Using district guidelines, survey students by grade level for SEL attributes and provide summary to staff for reflections and next steps.	November 2021
Professional Development	Incorporate feedback cycles.	Develop site peer observation schedule.	August 2021
College and Career	Infuse relevancy into lessons and practices.	Design a user-friendly method to allow teachers access to relevancy resources. Create a teacher sharing process for lesson ideas.	October 2021
Innovation	Use technology to enhance learning experiences.	Evaluate staff use of technology using the SAMR model and identify key areas of improvement.	September 2021

Student Learning Community (SLC) Starter Template

School Name: _____

Vision for Student Learning Communities: _____

Example Essential Questions	Considerations
What are the site-based essentials to developing a student collaborative culture?	Student ownership, learning partnerships, goal setting, data analysis
What processes need to be in place to measure collaboration, productivity, and student learning?	Continuum rubrics, growth progressions, identified standards-based targets
What are the behavioral expectations for SLCs?	SLC collective commitments, 21st Century Learning: Communication, Collaboration, Critical Thinking, Creativity
What specific growth progressions might your team use to measure SLC productivity?	Collaboration rubric, SEL essentials continuum, execution of roles and responsibilities rubric
What are the essential outcomes for SLCs?	Increased student performance, enhanced critical soft skills to work in team settings, solution-focused outcomes
What are the conditions we need to create within the classrooms to promote SLCs and ensure they function effectively?	Teacher attributes, teacher expectations, enthusiastic and exciting learning environment, nonthreatening environment, a spirit of collaborative (not solely competitive) exchanges
What are the essential characteristics of student-led learning? What does it look like? What does it sound like?	Student voice and choice, adherence to established norms, shared accountability, active engagement, productive struggle, problem solving, respectful disagreements
What are possible ways that we can use the SLC model within the school day?	Assessment data analysis, collaborative performance tasks, SEL incorporation

Collective Efficacy in a PLC at Work® © 2021 Solution Tree Press

SolutionTree.com • Visit **go.SolutionTree.com/PLCbooks** to download this free reproducible.

BUILDING AUTONOMY TO ENHANCE COLLECTIVE EFFICACY

"Control leads to compliance; autonomy leads to engagement."

—Daniel Pink

Trust is essential to all aspects of collective efficacy. In Bandura's (1997) original definition of collective efficacy—"a group's shared belief in its conjoint capability to organize and execute the courses of action required to produce given levels of attainment" (p. 477)—one can infer that trust must exist in self and others to obtain high-performing achievement results. In the absence of trust, belief is nonexistent within the teams, and execution of any sort will fall apart. Leaders cannot underestimate the influence that autonomy continues to have on efficacy within schools, if nurtured and managed correctly. It must be clear to school leaders that autonomy serves not only as a powerful indicator of collective efficacy but also as an essential ingredient to unlock motivational constructs such as effort and control, while enriching the spirit of innovation within teams and organizations.

In this chapter, we highlight the discoveries we made during two different experiences in building collective team efficacy. Sanger's quest to build a cohesive instructional framework led to the use of two different approaches between 2004 and 2018. One experience was built between 2006 and 2009 and focused on Explicit Direct Instruction (EDI) implementation. The second experience was built on Universal Design for Learning (UDL) and was born of the demand to meet the 2010 Common Core standards and occurred between 2013 and 2018. Both experiences led Sanger's leadership to learn various lessons; these distinctly different approaches led to the leadership's learning and understanding of the power of autonomy for building collective efficacy.

The Challenge: The Need for Autonomy as Well as an Instructional Framework

By 2006, Sanger's evolution as a district was quickly accelerating, and we were learning more about what we didn't know and understand about instruction. The saying "The more you know, the more you realize you have much to learn" couldn't have been truer in this experience. As we were becoming more skilled in identifying effective instructional practices through our PLC process, the lack of a district instructional framework was glaringly evident.

Teachers were being evaluated as "effective" or "ineffective" based on principal perceptions, assumptions, and beliefs about what good instruction looked like. Principals themselves ranged from strong to very weak in their abilities and understandings when it came to what were best instructional practices. From one classroom to another, teachers displayed different delivery models and different approaches. Some were very active and engaging, while others were passive and indirect. Student success was often the result of the teacher lottery, meaning the luck of the draw depending on which teacher a student was assigned. The variance in the quality of instruction was enormous, and the potential student learning outcomes often depended solely on the quality of the teacher. Our district could not guarantee an expectation of best practices when it came to an aligned instructional delivery system.

In spite of the strides we had made in building a new culture and a shared vision, we still lacked an understanding of what good instruction was, how it was defined, and what it looked like. This lack of clarity created an increasingly glaring gap in our ability to improve student achievement consistently across the district. As a result, we chose the path of building an instructional framework that would provide clarity and give us the consistency and cohesiveness we desperately needed. We chose to invest in Explicit Direct Instruction (EDI).

Explicit Direct Instruction (EDI) is a term that describes a strategic collection of research-based instructional practices. Sanger Unified chose to train principals and teachers in EDI and contracted with a local educational research company, DataWORKS, aimed at improving learning for all students. As we learned more about EDI, we quickly discovered the importance of focusing on essential outcomes rather than practitioner-preferred strategies, units, or methods of delivery. Our organization turned EDI into a very prescriptive, repetitive instructional routine. All lessons needed to have the same flow and included the following:

- An explicit, student-friendly, and standard-aligned objective (written and stated)

- Explicit steps to meet the objective (modeled and stated)
- Modeling (*I do, we do, you do*, explicitly delivered)
- Frequent *checks for understanding* (CFUs), timely and measured

The repetitive nature of the way Sanger constructed EDI lessons and forced delivery of EDI lessons led to many teachers and even students resisting EDI. Over time, the resistance grew into flat-out refusal to embrace the program.

The universal perspective from our teachers was that EDI eliminated teacher freedom, creativity, and engagement with some of their favorite units—the things that made teaching and learning fun for both students and staff, regardless of learning outcomes. In the mind of the practitioners, EDI eliminated their ability to choose *how* they taught. In their minds, the district had already identified the standards as the *what* to teach, and now the district was determining the *how* of instruction as well. District leadership rejected those arguments because of the drastic need to improve student achievement results. It was leadership's unwavering belief that in order to elicit massive change, our instructional delivery system required a coordinated, focused, and deliberate approach.

By 2013, teacher resentment still lingered with a feeling that EDI was a top-down decision forced on teachers. And it was no surprise that at the first chance teachers had to argue that EDI was ineffective for addressing the new 2010 Common Core standards, they did. Despite the benefits created by having a cohesive instructional program, teacher teams still struggled with the perceived lack of choice and autonomy in their instructional decision making. The residue of EDI remained in the psyche of teams long after its introduction in 2006.

The Change

Universal Design for Learning (UDL) is a long-studied instructional framework for meeting the needs of all students. Its significance became apparent in California with the March 2015 publication of the California Statewide Task Force on Special Education report, in which the "Evidence-Based School and Classroom Practices" section called out two frameworks that would focus on meeting the needs of all learners: a multi-tiered system of support (MTSS) and Universal Design for Learning (UDL; California Statewide Task Force on Special Education, 2015). The organizational challenge Sanger faced was how to systematically roll out an implementation plan given what we had learned from our EDI experience. Our approach this time was different in that we wanted to create autonomy for teams in how they chose to engage with the new framework, in the hope of building a more lasting commitment to the framework among teacher teams. Primary to the commitment was that autonomy would enhance the efficacy of teams to implement, refine, and improve their instructional practices.

We set out by asking for volunteer teams—early adopters—who would be willing to lead the learning of the new framework. We hired a lead teacher for the district whose job it was to support these teams, and we made no compliance agreements for implementation. We simply asked teams to learn and share. Accountability for learning was the centerpiece for implementation—essentially, our "tight." The organization's view fundamentally changed. Accountability and learning were now bonded together, as opposed to naïvely being viewed as separate, independent pieces of improvement.

This new approach changed our district's commitment to the UDL framework. Over the next three years, we had more and more teams signing on to simply learn more about the framework. The early adopters influenced the adopters, and those adopters influenced the late adopters. Anthony Muhammad (2009) describes the level of staff acceptance on a scale, from *believers* (those who accepted a student-centered paradigm) to *fundamentalists* (those who protect the status quo). The model seen in figure 5.1 shows the percentage of staff that tend to fall into each category of acceptance. This model was developed around social changes in society and is now widely used as a basis of market research (Zuieback, 2012). It allows organizations to see the general distribution of people's beliefs when adopting a new idea (though, of course, it may change depending on the idea or change event in question).

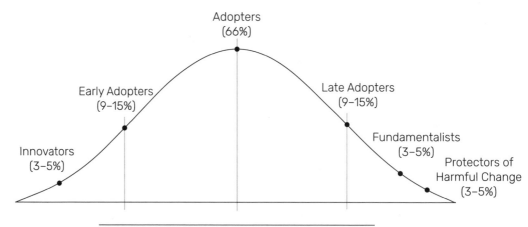

Figure 5.1: Understanding staff acceptance.

The innovators and early adopter teams at Sanger became the lead learners (learners or teachers) and key supports for other teams. Our principals were asked to simply learn and ask teams to apply and share what they had learned about the new framework with other teams. The teams shared their learning and explained how to best address learning needs for students using the framework. We showcased team improvements, putting highly effective teams on display so that they could pave the way for new teams. We defined our highly effective teams as those teams that exhibited the following.

- A willingness to try a new idea, strategy, or concept
- A willingness to fail and learn quickly and implement new strategies
- An ability to share ideas and track student progress
- A willingness to share concepts, resources, and planning tools for others to use

By the end of five years, virtually every school and at least one member from nearly every team was doing some form of UDL instructional delivery and learning with the UDL instructional framework. Almost every principal was able to showcase a staff member in every grade level who was using UDL as a way of bridging instructional learning gaps. The results from state student achievement results showed that, as a district, we continued to outpace other surrounding districts and perform above the state averages in both English language arts and mathematics. However, this time around, we had an instructional framework that was growing in staff commitment instead of resistance.

PRACTITIONER PERSPECTIVE

"It wasn't that I didn't appreciate all that EDI provided us as teachers, and more importantly the success for our students. What I resented was the way it was pushed on us with little opportunity to choose otherwise. Not only did the district tell us what to teach, now they wanted to tell us how to teach it, and I, along with others, resented that notion. UDL gave us an opportunity to build our skills, learn, and improve without fear of failure, retribution, or shame."

—Christy Platt
Former First-Grade Teacher, Now Principal,
Reagan Elementary

Leadership Paradoxes

The specific leadership paradoxes Sanger's leadership encountered when building autonomy to enhance collective efficacy were:

- Control vs. choice
- Autonomy vs. boundaries

Control vs. Choice

In his book *Smarter, Faster, Better: The Secrets of Being Productive in Life and Business*, Charles Duhigg (2016) highlights the work of a group of Columbia University psychologists and their contribution to the journal *Trends in Cognitive Sciences* (2010). The journal article identifies that when individuals or teams believe they are in *control*, they tend to work harder and push themselves more. In addition, they are more confident and overcome setbacks faster (Duhigg, 2016). People's beliefs are constructed based on their perceptions. The perception of control provides empowered choices and leads to greater teamwork. When teams can choose their paths, right or wrong, they are more likely to work harder to make the choice successful.

Duhigg (2016) asserts that the way to prove you are in control is to have *choice* over decisions: "Each choice—no matter how small—reinforces the perceptions of control and self-efficacy" (p. 19). Autonomy, choice, and the voice of teams embedded in organizational practices and culture lead to increased self- and collective efficacy. Duhigg (2016) highlights the notion that even if a decision delivers no benefit, people still want the freedom to choose. Further, Duhigg (2016) echoes the point made by Leotti and Delgado (2011) when they noted that "animals and humans demonstrate a preference for having a choice over not having a choice, even when that choice confers no additional reward" (p. 1310). The PLC process allows autonomy and choice by incorporating loose elements into the process. Specifically, the PLC process calls for loose leadership in how teachers deliver instruction (DuFour et al., 2016). Therefore, leaders may consider ensuring both choice and voice are embedded in all facets of the organization to allow genuine decision making and collaboration to be part of the culture.

In addition, research clearly states that autonomy actually translates to ownership across organizational systems if implemented with fidelity. In his book *Nuance*, Michael Fullan (2019) points out that "it is neither natural nor effective to motivate humans through surveillance" (p. 99). Although we recognize that leadership accountability sometimes requires direct action and one-dimensional decision making, we would contend that in most cases, top-down approaches of monitoring do not work. However, engaging in processes that build elements of self-regulation, choice, and autonomy contributes to transformation changes within cultures.

Kanold (2011) also recognizes the importance of autonomy in a different way, noting tiers of accountability. He references continuous improvement by engendering "an environment that favors vision speak over victim speak" (p. 53). This notion recognizes the value of moving from a vertical accountability model to one of self-accountability. Pink (2009) reinforces this idea, stating "this era doesn't call for better management. It calls for a renaissance of self-direction" (p. xi).

Although we used more substantial time and resources to roll out the framework of UDL with more team choice and autonomy around how to engage, we found the long-term impact of commitment outweighed the time, cost, and resources to support a more collaborative implementation model.

Autonomy vs. Boundaries

Loose–tight leadership is a never-ending balancing act. Although this balance often poses a significant challenge, it is imperative that the actions and energy in this space are non-negotiable for leaders. Kanold (2011) and Marzano and Waters's (2009) work intersects, drawing parallels within loose–tight leadership. In their research, they describe the need for leaders to find balance between defined autonomy and being a defender of boundaries. *Defined autonomy* means that school leaders are expected to lead within the boundaries of the district vision and goals. Leaders are expected to be *boundary defenders* to ensure the alignment of the most critical and coherent work defined by the district. These defined autonomy boundaries were actually shown to create less variance and increase the reliability of adult actions that improve students' achievement.

Essentially, it comes down to this: Adults can work within a set framework and still have the freedom to choose. Eliminating autonomy for teams translates to taking their independence and control away from their environment. In his book *The Five Disciplines of PLC Leaders*, Kanold (2011) points out, "Autonomy is different than independence" (p. 48). Autonomy is about balancing freedom of choice over how to proceed with meeting the expectations of the district or school vision (Kanold, 2011). According to Daniel Pink (2009), "Autonomy does not refer to going at it alone or freedom to do whatever we want. Autonomy can actually exist within a framework" (p. 90).

The pressing challenge was how we balance the desire for team autonomy with the district's desired direction for change. The PLC process gave our teams a form and function as we grew in the work. As our team capabilities grew, we were able to give our teams greater autonomy and choice on how they improved as teams. Leadership balanced the power of teams to choose how to engage with the instructional framework with the district's idea of how to build an instructional framework. In both experiences, we chose to be explicit in what we expected, and with UDL, we chose to be explicit with what we hoped they would learn and share. This led us to eventually having to accept that the paths we chose for EDI and UDL were both right and wrong. Meaning, the balance between autonomy and coherence is measured in small details that can contribute to bringing the system into equilibrium or tip the system toward instability. Both experiences were balanced at the time, and both created learning that helped teams evolve. However, we believe from our experience that both (UDL and EDI) represented autonomy in a different way, which ultimately fit the current demands for change. EDI was at a time when the organization *needed* to change; UDL came at a time when the organization *wanted* to change. Both had their role and place in Sanger's development.

Leadership Research

The following research helps to complement and build on the paradoxes Sanger's leadership discovered in the challenge. The paradox of discoveries leads us to consider research that either complements or challenges what we learned.

We reviewed research for the following themes:

- Integrity reflects values
- Vulnerability-based trust

Integrity Reflects Values

Integrity generally means adherence to a code or moral values. Integrity is essentially the practice of being honest and showing consistency. In ethics, integrity is regarded as the honesty and truthfulness or accuracy of one's actions. Sanger learned that the integrity with which our organization operated was based on the values we individually and collectively held. As Timothy Kanold (2011) says, "In the best PLC cultures, vision and values ultimately become the driving force behind the decision-making process that takes place every day" (p. 13). The key to values impacting the organization in a positive way is that people have to "live by them, reinforce them every day, and not tolerate behavior that is at odds with them" (Bryant, 2014, as cited in DuFour et al., 2016, p. 43).

We learned that as integrity was built around honoring the way teams chose to engage with the work, collective efficacy increased. As collective team efficacy improved, we were able to engage more teams with UDL. We had to infuse integrity into our methodology as well as our collaborative teams. Collaborative teams "engage in a systematic process in which they work together, interdependently, to analyze and impact their professional practice in order to improve individual and collective results" (DuFour et al., 2016, p. 60), and our desire for an effective instructional framework was essential for our teams to be able to analyze their practices. How could we expect teams to share practices and analyze results if, at the end of the day, they all taught what they wanted, when they wanted, and, most importantly, how they wanted?

By focusing on the integrity of teams— trusting that they would engage with our instructional framework and creating a driving force to autonomy—we were able to move away from compliance and monitoring and toward self-improvement and reflection. As DuFour et al. (2016) point out, organizations that understand their purpose and direction, and pledge to act, "don't need prescriptive rules and regulations to guide their daily work" (p. 41). DuFour et al. (2016) assert that when organizations implement this with true fidelity, "Policy manuals and directives [are] replaced by commitments and covenants" (p. 41). The fact that Sanger valued the fundamental purpose of team integrity gave our teams a sense of empowerment and commitment to a new framework unlike any we had experienced with other initiatives.

Vulnerability-Based Trust

"Dysfunctional teams prefer artificial harmony to insightful inquiry and advocacy" (DuFour et al., 2016, p. 71). This "artificial harmony" that DuFour and colleagues describe provides a false sense of security detrimental to the organization. Teams that contrive and manufacture these plays on invincibility are endangering the fabric of the collective efficacy. The truth is that teams with a high degree of integrity operate with a greater sense of trust. They are unafraid to discuss shortcomings or challenges, as they know that the clear truths of realities are a necessity for growth. Overcoming this level of dysfunction requires teams to consider vulnerability. Organizations create vulnerability in systems when they are more interested in what teams learn than in teams following their strict implementation directions. In other words, when an organization is focused on learning, they have to accept that teams may discover something that contradicts what they had hoped to discover. And the organization's ability to step away from their focused hope is vulnerability at its core.

Patrick Lencioni (2002) asserts that the best way to build a high-performing team is through vulnerability-based trust. This translates to teams communicating mistakes and exposing weaknesses to their colleagues in the spirit of improvement. Lencioni (2002) verifies that being vulnerable is actually a sign of strength within school organizations. In order for teams to be truly interdependent, teams require vulnerability and the reliance of team members on one another to improve the practices of all.

This level of authenticity requires individuals to overcome the fear of genuinely sharing their authentic self and actions with the teams. A healthy school culture will allow authenticity to be part of the ecosystem. It will not allow for the false narrative that individuals who expose vulnerabilities will be viewed by teams as failures or branded as inadequate. DuFour et al. (2006, 2010) point out that the best way for leaders to navigate this is through modeling. Leaders must allow themselves to be vulnerable by encouraging a learning spirit, not an artificial storyline and dog-and-pony show as a portrait of perfection. Leaders must create a culture that encourages open dialogue, without judgment, where teams can address discrepancies in practices.

REFLECTION QUESTIONS

At this point, stop to consider the paradoxes and research mentioned in the previous sections. Take a moment to answer the following questions to help create further awareness for your own team and organizational collective efficacy.

continued ⇨

1. What *situations* does your team face that are opportunities for creating autonomy within your team or organization?

2. What *questions* does your team need to ask to uncover perceptions about team autonomy within your team or organization?

3. What *beliefs and convictions* exist that may deter your team or organization from infusing more autonomy into the team or organization?

Now that you have considered these questions in relation to your own organization, we will share with you the leadership lessons that Sanger learned in their experience of building autonomy to enhance collective efficacy.

Leadership Lessons on Autonomy

In this section, we present our learnings from both the challenge story we experienced at Sanger Unified School District and the research previously presented. We attempt to bring together the challenge, the paradoxes we shared, and what the research asks us to consider in specific examples.

The leadership lessons we discuss in this section are:

- Evolution requires rethinking and reinvesting.
- Discover integrity.
- Trust is the bridge.

Evolution Requires Rethinking and Reinvesting

What Sanger gained from using a new approach for building autonomy was extraordinary commitment and efforts from teams to learn the new UDL framework. Teachers chose when to learn and how to begin trying out the new instructional framework. We rejected the "surveillance" model—the helicopter compliance and monitoring that so often are a way to guarantee implementation with a complex system—which dramatically helped reduce the anxiety for teams during implementation.

UDL took us longer to implement than EDI, and as a result, we had to work through the fog of implementation, testing the collective resolve and commitment to the *learning by doing* approach. Overall, even though we labored to find out what strategies and principles of UDL were most effective, we built team efficacy through the freedom of autonomy about *how* and *when* to engage in the work. This eventually led to large-scale changes and renewed our teams' sense of ownership. As a result, we had greater teacher team commitment and sustainability with UDL than we ever had with EDI.

As we reflect on our case study, there is a clear and obvious notion that leadership disregarded autonomy in the instructional framework for EDI. However, at this point in the district's evolution, there was a desperate sense of urgency to respond to the organization's dysfunction with overwhelming force and clarity.

The tight, suffocating directives of EDI proved costly. We had achieved a shameful perception from practitioners that we had forced EDI on teachers and students. Eventually, when staff had a chance to move away from the approach, they immediately and joyfully did—and not because it was a poor framework. In fact, most teachers today would argue that teams have kept many essential components of EDI as part of their instructional design. The simple fact that collaborative teams could achieve autonomy by choosing to do away with EDI led many to abandon the approach.

In rethinking how to approach the work, we realized we had to make a different investment in PLCs and UDL. Our teams had to evolve with the times, and as a result, so did our approaches. Our new approaches had to be less about telling people what to do and how to do it, and more about giving our teams flexibility to learn and understand. Our tight had to be broad, and our loose had to be even broader. We had to reevaluate our loose–tight for teams as being more flexible and yet more specific. We had to expand our timelines for implementation and honor the time for collective learning of teams above all other accountability options.

Discover Integrity

The reward for autonomy had to be earned, not given. Our work with teams showed that our leaders were willing to trust but also needed to verify that teams were actually doing the work. That is when we noticed that the measure of a team's ability to self-regulate its own collective commitments was held in a team's attributes—specifically, integrity as a measure of the team's personality. And when a team struggled, it most often came down to the team's integrity. Could they be trusted to make an attempt at learning, hold to the "tight" agreements, and hold themselves accountable to the defined outcomes? This degree of integrity had a larger dedication to the team's collective commitments that would form the positive habits they needed to build collective team efficacy.

Our journey of building collective efficacy now included the realization that teams existed with varying degrees of integrity. Our leaders couldn't be everywhere at once. Collaborative teams had to be able to work independently, and over time, it became clear that with some teams, the work wasn't a "skill" conversation, it was a "will" conversation. Some teams were simply not willing to attempt to try something new for the sake of learning. They wanted to be left alone and to choose for themselves how to engage when they wanted to engage. Having identified, as an organization, what highly collaborative teams do, it was clear what we needed our teams to become. If we were going to move teams forward, we had to hold them accountable, not only to the process of creating collective commitments but also living them with integrity.

What we discovered was that autonomy is the reward for doing the right work. Integrity is a sense of confidence and honesty built from self-monitoring. This awareness helps reinforce that building team efficacy is a journey, not a destination. Periodically, it is important for leaders to check their teams' integrity. Having an integrity process naturally defuses strict compliance methods some organizations sometimes use to monitor team commitments and behaviors.

Checking a team's integrity helps teams, and the leaders of teams, measure their sustainability over time by focusing on the team's desired outcomes while being mindful of the importance of self-regulation. Teams that build internal accountability for the behaviors that matter most truly build higher degrees of collective team efficacy. Therefore, we ask that leaders consider becoming more intentional about the frequency of integrity checks to help build the collective team efficacy. A team's actual commitments to itself are as important to collective team efficacy as the four critical questions (DuFour et al., 2016) are to a PLC. We encourage teams to do an integrity check, three times a year, with direct questions that address the collective commitments that leaders believe reflect the core values of the team or organization.

The following are questions that allow leaders to begin a conversation related to integrity, self-monitoring, and autonomy. This is not a solution-seeking conversation but rather an integrity conversation anchored around team reflections.

- What is it about our collective commitments that is working for our team?
- What is it about our collective commitments that is not working for our team?
- Are we clear about our collective commitments, and is learning part of our work?
- Are we clear about the tight elements of our work and what we need to achieve?
- What do we need to change or adjust as a team in order to improve student achievement?

Reflecting on these questions can help teams intentionally focus on the integrity aspects of team efficacy that lead to team autonomy. Self-reflection allows the teams to anchor themselves in the behaviors that matter most.

Trust Is the Bridge

Connecting trust to collective efficacy is paramount for organizational success. Providing autonomy is one way that leaders can show trust in teams and team members. It is one of the constant contributing factors in high-performing organizations that is substantiated in extensive research (see, for example, Bloomberg & Pitchford, 2017; Covey, 2006; Kanold, 2011; Pink, 2009). In *The Speed of Trust*, Covey and Merrill (2006) emphasize it this way: "Contrary to what most people believe, trust is not some soft, illusive quality that you either have or don't; rather, trust is a pragmatic, tangible, actionable asset that you can create" (p. 2). Kanold, in *The Five Disciplines of PLC Leaders* (2011), asserts that in order to build trust, leaders must embrace the following principles:

- Trust begins with a personal commitment to respect others.

- Trust is built on kept promises.

- For trust to be sustained, you must demonstrate competence.

Additionally, Bloomberg and Pitchford (2017), in *Leading Impact Teams*, noted that "relational trust is key to building effective teams and an essential ingredient in building collective efficacy" (p. 19).

Trust in team members' commitment and capacity is essential for the health and culture of the school organization. This translates to team members feeling accepted, respected, and empowered. Trust is not one-dimensional by any means. It must be defined, earned, honored, and reciprocated. In addition, school organizations must foster trust in multiple directions: top-down, lateral, bottom-up, and diagonal. Much like a spiderweb must connect to many surfaces to form a strong union, trust must bridge the various parts and people of the organization for collective efficacy to thrive.

In 2016, the National Council of Professors of Educational Administration's (NCPEA) *Education Leadership Review* published a research study titled "Investigating the Role of Collective Trust, Collective Efficacy, and Enabling School Structures on Overall School Effectiveness" (Gray, 2016). The research uncovered powerful relationships between student achievement outcomes and the constructs that help bring a deeper understanding and appreciation for both the wins (successes) and losses (failures) during our tenure. The NCPEA endorsed the study for its role in furthering the scholarship and practice of school administration and K–12 education. The theoretical framework hypothesized that "overall school effectiveness was influenced individually and jointly by collective trust, collective efficacy, and enabling structures" (Gray, 2016, p. 114).

Trust directly and indirectly impacts school effectiveness. Patrick B. Forsyth, Curt M. Adams, and Wayne K. Hoy (2011) note, "Trust is defined as 'faculty's willingness to be vulnerable to another party based on confidence that the latter party is benevolent, reliable, competent, honest, and open'" (p. 35). Roxanne M. Mitchell, Jingping Sun, Sijia Zhang, Brenda Mendiola, and C. John Tarter (2015) conducted a meta-analytic review of research regarding school effectiveness. They conclude that "teacher trust was the most powerful predictor of school effectiveness" (Mitchell et al., 2015, p. 168). It is worth noting that Forsyth and colleagues' (2011) work acknowledges vulnerability as a vital component in developing trust; however, it is just as important to recognize its two dimensions. The first dimension includes a *willingness* to be vulnerable, while the second dimension includes a *confidence* in others to do the same. This was interesting for leaders because it became apparent that trust was more reciprocal than initially thought.

The NCPEA study (Gray, 2016) notes the close relationship between collective trust and collective efficacy. As a reminder, Bandura (1997) defines collective efficacy as "a group's shared belief in its conjoint capability to organize and execute the courses of action required to produce given levels of attainment" (p. 477). These shared beliefs in conjoint capability absolutely require trust. The NCPEA study (Gray, 2016) connects and reinforces Bandura's (1997) and Forsyth et al.'s (2011) findings, concluding that collective efficacy is a "strong determinant of trust" (p. 116). The NCPEA research also highlights that teachers with collective efficacy tended to reflect resiliency attributes and overcome challenges rather than allowing obstacles to hinder success. Finally, the study finds that perceived collective efficacy refers to the "judgment of teachers in a school"—that faculty can organize and execute the course of action required for students' success (Goddard et al., 2000).

Enabling structures that foster trust and autonomy are also powerful indicators of overall school effectiveness. Gray (2016) describes enabling school structures as teachers' belief that the administration and rules of the school support collective teacher work. Wayne K. Hoy and Scott R. Sweetland (2007) assert that schools with enabling structures "developed an atmosphere of trust and teacher commitment to their school and its mission" (p. 372). Enabling school structures are established upon hierarchies of authority and a system of rules that help rather than hinder the teaching and learning mission of the school (Hoy & Sweetland, 2000). Faculty in schools with enabling structures foster trust, value differences, enable cooperation, and encourage innovation (Hoy & Tschannen-Moran, 2003). It is important to note that enabling structures led to teachers viewing their schools as more effective at producing results aligned with leadership's established goals.

The implications of practice in the study were profound. Forsyth et al. (2011) outline four guidelines for practitioners.

1. Establish trust in the principal by being trustworthy.

2. Be a leader, sometimes a manager.

3. Expect, respect, and model organizational citizenship.

4. Develop and nurture a culture of trust and optimism.

Conclusion: Connecting Autonomy to Collective Efficacy

There is an obvious, strong correlation between the autonomy construct and collective efficacy within school organizations. A leader must carefully manage his or her use of autonomy as a tool. As is clearly pointed out in the research, autonomy is best utilized within some boundaries or structures; without them, organizations will falter. In addition, the freedom to choose and navigate processes or procedures, instructional strategies, or collaboration methods is key to success, but without integrity, choice is futile.

School leaders may want to consider the following when attempting to build autonomy to enhance trust and collective efficacy:

- Consider the risk and reward of autonomy within systems.

- Consider your current organizational state. Does it require immediate change to expand or limit autonomy?

- Consider opportunities where choice (autonomy) can exist.

- Consider "integrity checks" with teams to measure the clarity of understanding and genuine level of implementation.

- Consider creating conditions that foster ongoing trust while instituting systems that verify and ensure fidelity of practices that lead to improved student achievement.

Next Steps

In this section, we provide some simple next steps associated with the learnings from the readings.

- Use the "1–5–10 Assessment Tool: Autonomy" reproducible (page 106) to assess autonomy within your school or organization.

- Read "Loose vs. Tight" by Richard DuFour (2016), published in *AllThingsPLC Magazine*, to better understand how to structure organizational autonomy.

- Use the "Staff Tight and Loose Template" reproducible on page 107, and the completed template provided, to better describe and organize autonomy for teams.

1–5–10 Assessment Tool: Autonomy

Assess and score each of the ten statements, with 1 being the lowest and 10 being the highest. Then calculate your total score.

Autonomy	Score
Teams embrace autonomy as freedom within boundaries or expectations.	1–5–10
Autonomy is honored within a framework of instructional expectations.	1–5–10
Autonomy is honored within a framework of assessment expectations.	1–5–10
Autonomy is honored within a framework of collaborative expectations.	1–5–10
Choice, intentionally built into the organization culture, strengthens collective commitments.	1–5–10
Autonomy and choice strengthen organizational culture.	1–5–10
Leaders honor autonomy by frequently and intentionally building structures and processes that allow teams to choose.	1–5–10
Leaders honor the power of voice for teams when making decisions by frequently consulting members.	1–5–10
Leaders frequently seek input from team members to guide and direct schoolwide organizational initiatives.	1–5–10
Teams fully understand the "tight" expectations of the work and honor the boundaries outlined by leadership.	1–5–10
Teams fully understand the "loose" flexibilities of the work and honor the creativity allowed by leadership.	1–5–10
Total points (maximum possible: 100)	

Collective Efficacy in a PLC at Work® © 2021 Solution Tree Press

SolutionTree.com • Visit **go.SolutionTree.com/PLCbooks** to download this free reproducible.

Staff Tight and Loose Template

Purpose:

The four critical questions of a PLC:

1. What do we want our students to learn?

2. How will we know when they have learned it?

3. What will we do when they don't learn it?

4. What will we do if they already know it?

Tight Aspects	**Loose Aspects**
Team Commitments:	Team Commitments:
Learning Goals:	Learning Goals:
Student Results:	Student Results:
Instructional Strategies:	Instructional Strategies:
Team Attendance:	Team Attendance:
Student Engagement:	Student Engagement:

page 1 of 2

Purpose:

To ensure that ALL students have access to high-quality, targeted learning while learning from home, and to ensure consistent, high-quality practice across all learning areas and grades

The four critical questions of a PLC:

1. What do we want our students to learn?

2. How will we know when they have learned it?

3. What will we do when they don't learn it?

4. What will we do if they already know it?

Tight Aspects	Loose Aspects
Team Commitments: Teams commit to developing and adhering to team commitments that support positive and healthy collaboration and dialogue. Teams will make commitments visible as a reminder.	**Team Commitments:** Teams will determine their own team commitments to support positive and healthy collaboration and dialogue. Teams can choose how best to make commitments visible.
Learning Goals: Teams should define essential standards, skills, and knowledge. Teams should define how students will be learning and how learning will be demonstrated and measured across the team .	**Learning Goals:** Teachers can choose which essential standards, skills, or knowledge they focus on Teams can develop their own tools, rubrics, and assessment for learning.
Student Results: All teams should have established targets for learning outcomes. All students and parents should have access to their results in a timely and coordinated way.	**Student Results:** Staff should define learning goals based on agreed-upon team objectives. Teams can use the most effective means possible for informing students and parents.
Instructional Strategies: Teams should prioritize the high-leverage practices (HLPs) they agree will be most effective for each lesson or unit.	**Instructional Strategies:** Teams can determine which HLPs they use.
Team Attendance: Staff will be on time and attend all PLC meetings.	**Team Attendance:** Teams can set start and end locations for team meetings.
Student Engagement: Staff will use active engagement strategies to build quality instructional lessons.	**Student Engagement:** Teams may choose which active engagement strategies they will use to maximize learning for students.

page 2 of 2

Collective Efficacy in a PLC at Work® © 2021 Solution Tree Press

SolutionTree.com • Visit **go.SolutionTree.com/PLCbooks** to download this free reproducible.

CHAPTER 6

BUILDING COLLABORATION TO ENHANCE COLLECTIVE EFFICACY

"Collaborative cultures, which by definition have close relationships, are indeed powerful, but unless they are focusing on the right things, they may end up being powerfully wrong."

—Michael Fullan

Collaboration requires evaluation and reflection of effective practices. Collaboration is not something you do as a result of a process; it is the process by which teams and team efficacy are built. Hattie (2012) states, "We need to collaborate to build a team working together to solve the dilemmas in learning, to collectively share and critique the nature and quality of evidence that shows our impact on student learning" (p. 151).

In this chapter, we highlight the discoveries and learnings that occurred at Sanger between 2004 and 2013. It was difficult for leaders to understand why some teams struggled and failed to have collaborative conversations. The district had built a sustainable foundation of understanding for the implementation of the PLC process that was far beyond what they ever could have imagined at the onset of implementation. Teams knew and understood how to function within a PLC and what the evidence of strong collaboration looked like but struggled to manage the threats to the collaboration that had taken so much time to build.

The Challenge: The Threats to Collaboration

Since 2004, Sanger Unified's district leadership had worked to understand and follow the steps of building a PLC process and had endeavored to build a sense of commitment to the learning with a singular focus of establishing a foundation of collaboration. Yet there still remained teams that struggled to achieve positive outcomes. Eventually, we came to realize and learn that struggling teams were hindered by three things that essentially paralyzed effective collaboration and collective team efficacy: (1) relationships, (2) politics, and (3) decision making.

Relationships

Relationships among staff were key to teams' ability to collaborate effectively, and there was no better evidence of a team that struggled to build collaborative structures than at Sanger's high school. For anyone who has ever worked at, or closely with, a high school, there comes a realization that high schools have their own unique relationships, politics, and decision-making structures. Because of the size and the focus on content by individual content-oriented teachers, high schools are often vastly different from middle and elementary schools in the way staff develop and maintain relationships. Relationships at the high school level occur by content area, and often those content-area teacher teams are large and have multiple members who may teach specific content within the department. This often leads to relationships being cursory or broken down into small silos of specific topics within content areas. For example, you might have an English department team, and within that department you might have AP English, English 9, English 10, English Comp, and so on. This presents a unique challenge when trying to bring teams together around common goals, common pacing, and common grading, all of which complicate the ability to build collective team efficacy.

The complexities of how teams create relationships further complicate teams' abilities to build collaborative structures and bonds. Often large high schools produce bifurcated teaming, where content-specific teams work in parallel with one another but not together, and that makes department decision making more complicated. As an example, imagine an English department, composed of the various sections described previously, trying to make a decision on determining critical essential standards for English. How do they integrate standards and determine assignment completion rating standards? How is AP English different from English 9, and how do the expectations change as a result? In the end, the issues that are often less complicated for elementary and middle school are more complicated at a high school.

Politics

Politics further complicates collaboration. Sanger's high school has over 150 teaching staff members, an amount five to six times larger than the feeder elementary sites and double that of the district's typical middle school. In many cases, the high school collaborative teams were as large as twelve or fourteen people, while in other cases the teams (such as those relating to electives, like fine arts and career and technical education) were as small as two or three people. A major contributing factor to the success or failure of teams extended beyond just the relationships of the individuals on the team and more to the *politics* of the team—namely, the ways in which the teams governed and made decisions for themselves. The political dynamics of the team were often determined by factors such as who influenced decision making, which classes teachers were assigned to teach, seniority preferences, union voices, or which staff were the loudest or had the ear of the department chairs.

The political landscape of some department teams required the team leader to display special leadership skills and strategies to navigate the complexity of department politics. The team leads were often charged with reshaping the prominent political dynamics of their department by giving voice to all team members to negate the political affiliations, power structures, and patterns that had been established historically. To complicate this dynamic of the political climate and culture of our departments, the department chairs, whose overall decision-making authority had been the norm, were not aligned with those who served as the collaborative team leads. The dangerous political precedent of not intentionally and explicitly defining the roles and responsibilities of the department chair and the team leaders provided an environment ripe for political conflict.

Decision Making

Decision making complicated our team leaders' ability to collaborate and build collective team efficacy. Often the true decision maker at a high school was the department head, and often, the team lead and the department head were two separate individuals. As a result, team leaders and department heads would frequently clash over defining the consensus and agenda of the team. As teams tried to have discussions about improving their instructional practices, it was often the department head that made things difficult, by overruling decisions or moving the conversation to more pressing issues.

Essentially, the department head was the decision maker both in title and in the mind of the administration. This dichotomy set up challenges with politics, relationships, and decision making. So what happens when the department head is not the collaborative team leader? Well, if these two individuals don't get along, then the ability to collaborate as a team is much more complicated. And that is exactly what we experienced in some departments at Sanger High School.

The structure and culture of one particular department presented some unique challenges. Up until 2004, when the district began its work with the PLC process, it was the department head who made decisions about the direction, collaboration, and decision of the team. It was often the most senior teacher who was awarded the title of department head. Teachers who volunteered to be collaborative team leads usually had less experience and were more willing to take on new roles and responsibilities. For example, one of our department heads had been in his position for over ten years. He had a reputation for being incredibly detailed and always crunching the numbers during negotiations, and to be quite frank, the team trusted his numbers during negotiations much more than they did the business department or even the superintendent.

This department head was well respected and had been part of the structure of the department for some time. The problem was, he didn't want to be the collaborative team lead, and he didn't necessarily believe in PLCs or the work the district had engaged in to build a collaborative PLC team structure. He was what Anthony Muhammad (2018) would call a *fundamental resister* when it came to collaboration, or what we would call a "protector of harmful change" (recall figure 5.1, page 94). Eventually, the organization failed to keep the difficulties of collaboration simple. We struggled to adequately prepare our collaborative team leads to effectively manage the complicated nature of team relationships, politics, and the decision making that they would undoubtedly encounter.

The short version of the story, as you can probably imagine, is that the relationships between the department heads and the collaborative team leads in some departments eroded over time because of the aforementioned issues. In some departments, the conflicts and dysfunctions began to create isolation and resentment between team members. These silos were born out of unfortunate politics. Those who resented the decisions of the department head over the course of time had an opportunity to consider the new collaborative team lead as the primary decision maker of the team. However, the possibility for redirection was suffocated by the inertia of the status quo—namely, that department heads wanted to lead teams and make decisions. Those who feared retribution gravitated back to the department head as the ongoing lead decision maker of the team. We ended up with further divided departments that could not function effectively and made few collaborative decisions work.

As Sanger's leadership, we could have eliminated a myriad of factors to better support the progress of collaborative structures for our high school teams. Not only could we have considered different approaches with team relationships and hierarchies, we also could have acted with additional strategies and directives. The district could have intervened with a higher degree of intensity that may have helped deter stronger individual personalities from drowning out other team members' thoughts and opinions. Confrontation was a necessary evil at this point, one Lencioni (2002) would highlight as one of the five dysfunctions of a team. Our understanding led us to believe that confrontation was part of the process, but we failed to act intentionally to guide the dysfunctions with such complexities as the high school. Not even the coach assigned to that team had a chance of breaking through the deep-rooted issues within the departments.

The Change

 By 2010, we had achieved no better collaborative structures or team efficacy, and it wasn't until some of the department chairs retired that the organization began to see change. That was unfortunate, in that we had come to realize our own misguided assumptions and mistakes. We hadn't provided clarity of responsibilities for collaborative team leads and department chairs, and we hadn't navigated the politics of a seniority-based system that created barriers to building effective teams. Most noticeably, we recognized that we had spent more time hiring an assistant football coach than selecting teachers, department heads, or collaborative team leads. It was only upon this revelation—that retirement was our unfortunate solution—that we started being more intentional about the team efficacy and collaboration leaders had so desperately desired. There was a harsh reality for some leaders, a sort of covert stonewalling, that prevented systemwide change from occurring. Barricading behavior from teachers inhibited progress at every turn. These individuals created unnecessary obstructions for team members and leadership, and resisted fundamental change to suit their very own beliefs and values. Our case study brings to life the true complexity of collaborative teams that influences collective efficacy: relationships, politics, and decision making.

PRACTITIONER PERSPECTIVE

"In retrospect, the PLC journey provided Sanger High School an opportunity to empower teachers who worked directly with the students on a daily basis to improve student achievement, as opposed to creating some type of ad hoc leadership committee or focus group in charge of impacting student performance. The reality of having both department heads and collaborative team leads complicated our ability to build collaborative structures that enhanced efficacy. Specifically, we learned that the solutions to the complexities of the high school setting were forged in the strategic formation of teams."

—Dan Chacon
Former Principal of Sanger High School, 2000–2019

Leadership Paradoxes

 The specific leadership paradoxes Sanger's leadership encountered when building collaboration to enhance collective efficacy were:

- Collaboration vs. co-laboring

- Implementation vs. adoption

Collaboration vs. Co-laboring

In *Learning by Doing, Third Edition*, there is a key principle for working with and in collaborative teams: true teams are those that have a shared understanding that a collaborative team is one that "work[s] interdependently to achieve a common goal for which members are mutually accountable" (DuFour et al., 2016, p. 60). Merriam-Webster defines *collaborate* as "to work jointly with others or together especially in an intellectual endeavor" ("Collaborate," n.d.). Peter M. DeWitt (2018) recognizes the broad scale of interpretation for what *collaboration* actually means. DeWitt (2018) notes the spectrum of shallow translations for collaboration, ranging from "working together with their sleeves rolled up, making one idea stronger" (p. 14) to cringing as they think of another pointless meeting where their voices don't matter. Getting to the heart of collaborative leadership, DeWitt (2018) writes,

> I believe that our moral purpose as leaders is to challenge our long-held beliefs, build the collective efficacy of staff, help raise the self-efficacy of students and families, and create opportunities in which we learn together through collaboration and stronger school climate. (p. 14)

On the surface, most teams in our district looked as if they were deeply collaborating—or they would have, if not for one glaring problem. Not all teams were generating positive results at the rate we anticipated, and as a result, leaders and curriculum support providers (CSPs) were assigned to support struggling teams to help them maneuver through the difficulties that prevented team efficacy and team collaboration. Leaders struggled to clearly define what they were seeing and experiencing with teams and missed what DuFour and colleagues (2016) call to task: "A collection of teachers does not truly become a team until members must rely on one another to accomplish a goal that none could achieve individually" (p. 60).

As the organization watched and learned, we found the following: that the teams that were struggling to collaborate effectively had designed their work together more like a model of *co-laboring* than collaboration (DuFour et al., 2016).

We observed teams that were co-laboring as demonstrating the following behaviors:

- Working with others but not necessarily changing their individual practices

- Sharing ideas but not building consensus around what to collectively achieve

- Making decisions based on what was best for adults

- Leaving meetings without collective consensus of the team

Teams that were truly collaborating demonstrated the following behaviors:

- Being willing to sacrifice for the purpose and vision of the team
- Focusing on students and improving student achievement
- Making decisions that were student-based and student-centered
- Prioritizing professional (honest) communication and relationships
- Sharing instructional practices and pedagogy
- Leaving meetings with consensus of shared outcomes and deliverables

Ultimately, we found that the teams that struggled with building efficacy and collaboration had members who were not coached well or monitored effectively enough to build commitments necessary for improving team efficacy. Therefore, well-intended laborious action did not yield the benefits of true collaboration.

Implementation vs. Adoption

Research and experience taught the Sanger leadership to recognize not only the wide spectrum of implementation of collaboration but also the variation of the teams' abilities and needs shaped by personality dynamics. We had teams ranging from being followers of only the basic rules of the PLC process to being fully engaged in improving instructional practices for the greater good. It became clear that the complexity of needs was far greater than just the increased consistency across our teams.

Donohoo and Velasco (2016) choose to use the word "adopted" versus "implemented" to describe the level of ownership necessary for systemic change. *Adopted* is referred to as "embracing, or taken on" while *implemented* refers to "deployment of a plan" (Donohoo & Velasco, 2016, p. 15) that usually belongs to someone else. We needed teams to fully *adopt* our collaborative ideology into our practices. Steven Katz, Lorna M. Earl, and Sonia Ben Jaafar (2009) maintain, "For collaboration to be an enabler of the kind of meaningful professional learning that can impact on practices, it needs to be more than just an inventory of group-based activities that we hope will make a difference" (p. 45).

Teams that focus on adoption are more likely to experience success as a collaborative team as opposed to those who are focused on implementation for compliance and monitoring. Implementation can easily be mistaken as adoption, and as we struggled to support our teams, we often found that not only did struggling teams have a myriad of issues related to relationships, politics, and decision making, they also struggled with adoption of the new expectations.

Leadership Research

The following research helps to complement and build on the paradoxes Sanger's leadership discovered in the challenge. The paradox of discoveries leads us to consider research that either complements or challenges what we learned.

The challenge for our district leaders was how to respond when team collaboration was difficult. Our case study was complicated because the relationships, politics, and decision-making factors of history and practice created tremendous barriers for our teams. It was as if the system had paralyzed the team, making it difficult for teams to collaborate, share ideas, and make decisions.

We failed as an organization to not only build the capabilities of collaborative team leads but also empower them with the tools necessary to combat challenging circumstances. In other words, we didn't prepare appropriately for making the *art of collaboration* simple. According to W. Richard Smith (2015), in his book *How to Launch PLCs in Your District*, "district leaders cannot expect principals to teach, coach, and support others by simply handing them copies of *Learning by Doing*" (p. 30). Smith (2015) goes on to assert that "A single workshop or general training session provides an introduction but does little to support or sustain implementation" (p. 30). We would argue that the same principle of empowering site administration in PLC implementation that Smith (2015) references applies to empowering collaborative team leaders as well.

Additionally, Fullan and Quinn (2016), in their book *Coherence: The Right Drivers in Action for Schools, Districts, and Systems*, emphasize that school organizations that successfully apply what works "identify and establish the conditions that push and support deep implementation" (p. 5). This deep implementation requires coherence and an "action framework consisting of four components: focusing direction, cultivating collaborative cultures, deepening learning, and securing accountability" (Fullan & Quinn, 2016, p. 3). This means that Sanger, as an organization, needed to do more to empower collaborative team leaders in these four areas with specific training and resources that fostered growth. Without providing ongoing and sustainable opportunities to strengthen and hone the skills of our collaborative team leaders, we failed to empower leaders across the system to build collective team efficacy and collaboration.

Lastly, in their book *Strengths Based Leadership: Great Leaders, Teams, and Why People Follow*, Tom Rath and Barry Conchie (2008) focus on the four domains of leadership strength: (1) executing, (2) influencing, (3) relationship building, and (4) strategic thinking. *Executing* refers to a leader making things happen with a solution-focused approach. *Influencing* refers to the leadership voice that commands authority, exudes confidence, and ensures that all voices are heard. *Relationship building* refers to unifying teams, eliminating distractions, and leveraging connection and rapport to get the best out of teams. *Strategic thinking* means displaying tremendous analysis skills and being deliberate in assisting teams when considering future possibilities. As a school organization, we needed to inject a more methodical and measured approach to empowering collaborative team leaders by identifying individual strengths and team dynamics. A more specific, strength-based approach for collaborative team leaders would have created increased awareness, equipped them to acknowledge and apply their strengths, and promoted the important balance among teams. A strength-based approach would have galvanized collaborative team leaders to engage the nuances of leading teams that are often the purview of administration. This engagement would have allowed collaborative team leaders to better combat the threats of collaboration.

The complexity within a collaborative team when it comes to relationships, politics, and decision making is that the team's discussions lead to decisions about instructional strategies, planning, pedagogy, and assessments for student learning. Those are all complicated discussions for a team that is not ready for them, and they are even more complicated for a leader who may not have the influence of other, more seasoned members of the team. When collaboration is not built on a strong foundation of working, trusting, honest relationships, and communication, team efficacy will not come to fruition.

REFLECTION QUESTIONS

At this point, stop to consider the paradoxes and research mentioned in the previous sections. Take a moment to answer the following questions to help create further awareness for your own team and organizational collective efficacy.

1. What are the potential *politics* that you need to manage to enable your team or organization's PLC to be more effective?

2. What *relationships* may complicate or erode collaborative teams?

3. What is the *decision-making* structure for your collaborative teams? Is it consensus? Are there other decision structures?

Now that you have considered these questions in relation to your own organization, we will share with you the leadership lessons that Sanger learned in their experience of building collaboration to enhance collective efficacy.

Leadership Lessons on Collaboration

In this section, we present our learnings from both the challenge we experienced at Sanger Unified School District and the research previously presented. We attempt to bring together the challenge, the paradoxes we shared, and what the research asks us to consider in specific examples.

The leadership lessons we discuss in this section are:

- Understand the seven stages of team development
- Use High-Leverage Team Actions (HLTAs) to move highly effective teams

Understand the Seven Stages of Team Development

If Sanger was going to build capacity for collective efficacy in collaborative teams, we realized our measure of effectiveness of the past needed to evolve. We eventually found an opportunity to expand our understanding of PLCs at Work in the valuable trainings and workshops conducted by Solution Tree. The right people with the right information helped our organization chart a new path. At the core of our new collective learning was a deeper understanding of the seven stages of collaborative teams and the High-Leverage Team Actions (HLTAs) aligned to the four critical questions of a PLC (DuFour et al., 2016).

What we learned was exactly what we were missing to address the challenges our teams were facing. Our false solution was that eventually the resisters would retire, but while we tried to outlast our resisters, we lost good team leaders because we failed to help them navigate next steps to improve collaboration. Solution Tree introduced our instructional leaders and teams to the *seven stages of collaborative teams* through access to professional development and institutes (Graham & Ferriter, 2008; Kanold, 2011; see figure 6.1). Each stage detailed specific actions that collaborative teams need to take to ensure the integrity of the PLC process is upheld. The stages, defined in the following list, helped to quantify whether or not collaborative teams have the right focus and clarity.

- Stage 1—Filling in the Time
- Stage 2—Sharing Personal Practice
- Stage 3—Planning, Planning, Planning
- Stage 4—Developing Common Assessments
- Stage 5—Analyzing Student Learning
- Stage 6—Adapting Instruction to Student Needs
- Stage 7—Using the Continuous Learning Cycle

We immediately saw the flaws in our thinking as we attempted to enhance collective efficacy of our collaborative teams and build collaboration across our district.

The seven stages helped teams focus on the specific actions and behaviors that needed to improve so PLCs could experience success (see figure 6.1). The process gave teams a way to reflect on their current state, discuss the reasons why, collaborate on ways to improve, and position team coaches and site leaders to provide more focused supports and conversations.

	Stage and Questions That Define the Stage	Description of the Stage
Stage 1. Filling in the Time	• *What exactly are we supposed to do?* • *Why are we meeting?* • *Is this going to be worth my time?*	• Teams in this stage may believe in the PLC concepts but lack clear guidelines or experiences regarding what they need to focus on during collaboration time. • Team members believe that student learning is based primarily on student effort, motivation, and family conditions. • Teams have not explicitly identified what students should know, understand, and be able to do. • Team members have limited awareness of what and when other teachers are teaching, what they expect their students to learn, or how they assess that learning. • Teams in this stage typically struggle to fill time or move to the other extreme and try to accomplish too much, too quickly. • The site administrator is not clear about his or her expectations for the teams. • This stage is characterized by frustration, bewilderment, and a desire to go back to what was comfortable.
Stage 2. Sharing Personal Practice	• *What is everyone else doing in their classrooms?* • *What are some of the relevant activities you use for this unit?*	• Teachers have identified some key standards and have a general pacing plan, but there is limited mutual accountability. • Teams have not established collaboration time. • Teachers in this stage may be genuinely interested in what other teachers are doing, hoping to pick up new ideas. • Talking about teaching feels like collaboration but does not include the in-depth look at learning. • Teachers' opinions and decisions are not based on student learning results. • Conversations about practice are comfortable but rarely take the next step toward talking about student learning.

Source: Adapted from Graham & Ferriter, 2008; Kanold, 2011; Schuhl, 2018.

Figure 6.1: The seven stages of collaborative teams in PLCs.   continued ⇨

	Stage and Questions That Define the Stage	Description of the Stage
Stage 3. Planning, Planning, Planning	• *What content should we be teaching, and how should we pace this unit?* • *How do we lighten the load for each other?* • *Have we planned a "rich lesson" collaboratively?*	• Teachers utilize the team approach to plan together. Rather than each teacher individually planning every lesson, different members take responsibility for sets of lessons and share their planning work with others. • Unfortunately, teams often grow comfortable with shared planning and fail to focus on results. Teacher attention remains centered on teaching rather than learning.
Stage 4. Developing Common Assessments	• *How do you know students have learned?* • *What does mastery look like?* • *What does student proficiency look like?*	• Shared assessments force teachers to define exactly what students should learn and what evidence is necessary for documenting success. • Some team members may work to avoid common assessments, thereby steering clear of difficult conversations, but common assessments are essential if teams are to shift their focus from teaching to learning. • The site administrator expects data-driven teams to use progress monitoring.
Stage 5. Analyzing Student Learning	• *Are students learning what they are supposed to be learning?* • *What does it mean for students to demonstrate understanding of the learning targets?*	• Professional learning teams begin to shift their focus from teaching to learning. • Teachers spend time looking at and dissecting student work, analyzing the strengths and areas of improvement for each student. • Teachers use the assessment results to recommend student intervention and enrichments. • Teams may be very motivated in this stage and can be driven by results. However, teachers also encounter the delicate position of publicly facing the results of their classroom, which may elicit an intensely personal response. • Collective intelligence provides a never-ending source of solutions for addressing shared challenges.

	Stage and Questions That Define the Stage	Description of the Stage
Stage 6. Adapting Instruction to Student Needs	• *How can we adjust instruction to help those students struggling and those exceeding expectations?*	• Teachers, teacher leaders, and school leaders collectively commit to helping all students improve and learn. Behaviors in the teams represent this commitment. • Teams are typically performing at high levels, taking collective responsibility for student success rather than responding as individuals. They set SMART goals and revisit them periodically. • A major focus is on building the pyramid of interventions to be systematic and progressively more intense. Teams analyze core instruction and revise it if needed. • Teams use data to make decisions about providing initial instruction and tiers of intervention. • The site administrator is fully engaged in the processes.
Stage 7. Using the Continuous Learning Cycle	• *Which of our instructional and assessment practices are most effective with our students?*	• Teams embrace the "continuous learning cycle" and keep honing instruction and assessments. • This question brings the process of professional learning team development full circle, connecting learning back to teaching. • Teams are engaged in deep reflection, tackling innovative projects such as action research and lesson study. • In this stage, you will find teachers observing other classrooms, videotaping instruction, intentionally inviting others into the group, and "growing" the success of the team into a school culture. • Students within the classrooms are organized as "student learning communities" (SLCs) and share many of the same elements as teacher learning teams.

Use HLTAs to Move Highly Effective Teams

Although much of what we have shared thus far has focused on highlighting our failed attempts to improve ineffective teams, we want to ensure readers that the Sanger leadership did, in fact, address those teams and challenged ourselves with what to do next to support and improve highly effective teams. Using HLTAs created an opportunity to fill a gap in our ability to improve teams that were already on the right track, possessed a high degree of collective efficacy and effective practices, and for all intents and purposes were considered to be highly effective and efficacious teams. The HLTAs were a road map and a way for Sanger's leaders and coaches to provide more valuable strategic feedback for our effective teams than increased pressure, monitoring, accountability, and compliance around student score results.

The HLTAs helped teams reconsider the specific efforts they as a team needed to take to enhance team efficacy, and more specifically, how they were addressing the four critical questions of a PLC (DuFour et al., 2016). For example, a fourth-grade team, in relationship to mathematical fluency, might say, "We want all fourth-grade students to master 100 single-digit multiplication problems in four minutes or less." HLTAs break that goal down into considerations that occur before, during, and after the unit actions that teams need to consider and develop. See figure 6.2 for examples of HLTAs aligned to the four critical questions of a PLC.

The seven stages of collaborative teams and the High Leverage Team Actions provided Sanger's leadership with a clearer pathway to improve both effective and ineffective team collaboration.

Conclusion: Connecting Collaboration to Collective Efficacy

When one considers the research around collaboration and earnestly reflects on some of Sanger Unified's successes and shortcomings as an organization, it becomes clear that we as district leaders could have been more intentional about supporting site and teacher leaders in building team efficacy, especially at the secondary level. In spite of the challenges faced at the secondary level, Daniel Chacon, SHS principal for nearly twenty years, demonstrated exceptional leadership in guiding the politics, relationships and decision making. Experienced leadership is what bridged the complexities at high school and led SHS to extraordinary success, culminating in multiple state and national recognitions. In retrospect, it's helpful to consider the various and sometimes additional support mechanisms that are needed to address relationships, politics and decision making at the secondary levels:

- Appropriate coaching support for teacher leaders.
- Working below the green line with higher degrees of intentionality to foster an authentic collaborative spirit.

High-Leverage Team Actions	1. What do we want all students to know and be able to do?	2. How will we know if they know it?	3. How will we respond if they don't know it?	4. How will we respond if they do know it?
Before-the-Unit Team Actions				
HLTA 1. Making sense of the agreed-on essential learning standards (content and practices) and pacing	■			
HLTA 2. Identifying higher-level-cognitive-demand mathematical tasks	■	◧		
HLTA 3. Developing common assessment instruments	◧	■		
HLTA 4. Developing scoring rubrics and proficiency expectations for the common assessment instruments		◧		
HLTA 5. Planning and using common homework assignments	◧	■	◧	◧
During-the-Unit Team Actions				
HLTA 6. Using higher-level-cognitive-demand mathematical tasks effectively	◧	■		
HLTA 7. Using in-class formative assessment processes effectively	◧	◧	■	■
HLTA 8. Using a lesson-design process for lesson planning and collective team inquiry	■	■	■	■
After-the-Unit Team Actions				
HLTA 9. Ensuring evidence-based student goal setting and action for the next unit of study			■	■
HLTA 10. Ensuring evidence-based adult goal setting and action for the next unit of study			■	■

■ = Fully addressed with high-leverage team action

◧ = Partially addressed with high-leverage team action

Source: Adapted from Kanold et al., 2018.

Figure 6.2: Form to align HLTA to the four critical questions of a PLC.

Visit ***go.SolutionTree.com/PLCbooks*** *for a free reproducible version of this figure.*

- Cultivate the further development and alignment of perspectives to enhance genuine interdependence between district and secondary leaders.

- Create space and time to genuinely work alongside secondary leaders to help build capacity and coherence in an effort to produce greater outcomes for students.

In the end, Sanger High School's overall commitment to the PLC process, coupled with experienced leadership from Principal Chacon, provided the leverage necessary to build collaborative structures that led to enhanced beliefs and confidence amongst all levels of the organization, eventually leading to increased efficacy.

Next Steps

In this section, we provide some simple next steps associated with the learnings from the readings.

- Use the "1–5–10 Assessment Tool: Collaboration" on page 125 to assess collaboration within your school or organization.

- Consider the information on the seven stages of collaboration shown in figure 6.1 (page 119) to assess teams' levels of collaboration.

- If your team is ready for a more advanced level of collaboration, assess your team using the HLTAs (shown in figure 6.2, page 123) to determine more advanced opportunities to enhance collaboration.

- Consider using the reproducible "1–5–10 Assessment Tool: HLTAs" (page 126) specifically focusing on collaboration around HLTAs.

- To focus your teams' long-term commitments toward collective efficacy, use the "Collective Efficacy Focus Planning Tool" reproducible on page 127 to organize actions for improving team collaboration by prioritizing your most challenging areas from the 1–5–10 collaboration assessment tool.

1-5-10 Assessment Tool: Collaboration

Assess and score your organization on each of the ten statements, with 1 being the lowest and 10 being the highest. Then calculate your total score.

Team Collaboration	Score
Team focus is student centered in every meeting.	1–5–10
Team members are fully interdependent, relying on the team for support, resources, and solutions.	1–5–10
Teams address one of the four critical questions every meeting and hold each other mutually accountable.	1–5–10
Teams set and analyze SMART goals in every meeting.	1–5–10
Team members are organized and prepared each meeting to discuss the most recent data.	1–5–10
Teams review student learning data with the purpose of improvement of instructional practices.	1–5–10
Teams review common formative assessment results to improve instructional practice.	1–5–10
Teams review common formative assessment results to identify necessary student intervention or enrichment in every meeting.	1–5–10
Teams review common formative assessment results to place in necessary intervention activities to address critical question 3.	1–5–10
Teams review common formative assessment results to place in necessary enrichment activities to address critical question 4.	1–5–10
Total points (maximum possible: 100)	

Collective Efficacy in a PLC at Work® © 2021 Solution Tree Press

SolutionTree.com • Visit **go.SolutionTree.com/PLCbooks** to download this free reproducible.

1-5-10 Assessment Tool: HLTAs

Assess and score your organization on each of the ten statements, with 1 being the lowest and 10 being the highest. Then calculate your total score.

Team Collaboration	Score
HLTA 1: We have agreed-on essential standards, content, practice, and pacing.	1–5–10
HLTA 2: We have identified higher-level-cognitive-demand tasks.	1–5–10
HLTA 3. We have developed common assessment instruments.	1–5–10
HLTA 4: We have developed score rubrics and proficiency expectations.	1–5–10
HLTA 5: We plan with and use common homework assignments.	1–5–10
HLTA 6: We use higher-level-cognitive-demand tasks.	1–5–10
HLTA 7: We use in-class formative assessment processes effectively.	1–5–10
HLTA 8: We use a lesson-design process.	1–5–10
HLTA 9: We ensure evidence-based student goal setting.	1–5–10
HLTA 10: We ensure evidence-based adult goal setting.	1–5–10
Total points (maximum possible: 100)	

Collective Efficacy Focus Planning Tool

Which areas from the 1-5-10 collaboration assessment do we want to improve as a team?	Who will hold us accountable to our team improvement?	What potential threats exist that will derail our team collaboration goals?	What behaviors do we need to change or watch out for to protect us from the potential threats?

CHAPTER 7

MOVING FROM PARADOXES, RESEARCH, AND LEADERSHIP LESSONS TO A THEORY OF ACTION: BUILDING COLLECTIVE TEAM EFFICACY

"High reliability leadership is developing this capacity to focus on the right work and the discipline to sustain that work over time to deliver a highly reliable opportunity for learning."

—Philip B. Warrick

This chapter brings together the learnings and discoveries of the previous chapters into a Theory of Action (TOA) for how teams build collective team efficacy. Considering the paradoxes, research, and leadership lessons Sanger's leaders discovered during their transformation, we attempt to build a mental model of *what* and *how* we believe these constructs are interrelated to build collective efficacy. The TOA provides ways for leaders to assess their own teams' current states of efficacy in relation to the topics from each chapter. The TOA highlights experiences or conditions that leaders must create to move teams forward in building collective team efficacy. This TOA provides the foundation necessary to support the continued development and building of highly effective teams.

The Research

The phenomenal research and extensive work of John Hattie have illuminated a path for educators to consider collective teacher efficacy as a viable source to create positive organizational change and improve outcomes for students. According to Hattie (2018), "A school staff that believes it can collectively accomplish great things is vital for the health of a school, and if its members believe they can make a positive difference, they very likely will."

Hattie's research around collective teacher efficacy asks readers to understand not only the meaning behind positive effect sizes but also the relationship between collective teacher efficacy and its impact on student outcomes. In his investigations, Hattie developed a way to look at different meta-analyses according to their effect (or impact) on learning outcomes. In fact, Hattie (2017) ranked 252 influences and effect sizes related to student achievement. What he found was that collective teacher efficacy had a strong correlation with improving learning outcomes—an effect size of 1.57 (Hattie, 2018).

To understand the importance of the 1.57 effect size, we refer to *Building Behavior: The Educator's Guide to Evidence-Based Initiatives* by Jessica Djabrayan Hannigan and John E. Hannigan (2020). The authors explain Hattie's research as follows: an effect size of 1.0 would mean that, on average, students receiving that treatment would exceed 84 percent of students not receiving the treatment. If collective teacher efficacy has an effect size of 1.57, then it has a considerable impact on producing positive learning outcomes (Hannigan & Hannigan, 2020).

Hannigan and Hannigan (2020) also expand on Hattie's work by highlighting the effect size of d = 0.4, also known as the "hinge point." Factors with effect sizes greater than 0.4 fall into the "zone of desired effects" (p. 25), meaning that they have the greatest impact on student learning. Furthermore, the zone between d = 0.0 and d = 0.4 is what a student could achieve without schooling or by the simple process of maturation alone. Therefore, any effects below d = 0.4 are potentially harmful. A mean effect size of 1.57 is well beyond the "hinge point." This research reinforces our collective efforts to build and enhance collective teacher efficacy within school organizations. We have compiled these findings into our Theory of Action.

The Theory of Action and the Pyramid of Collective Efficacy

The Theory of Action is a mental model that captures Sanger's mental representation of collective teacher efficacy. Leaders may use this model to apply a working theory of improving collective team efficacy in their own school or district. Each of the chapters in this book highlight the various sources of influence, paradoxes, and belief constructs organizational leaders and teams must address when attempting to build more positive collective teacher efficacy. The TOA also identifies factors to consider when attempting to enhance efficacy while managing threats that may derail leadership efforts. Figure 7.1 shows the interplay between these concepts—the source of influence, paradox, and belief constructs—that affect leadership's ability or inability to build collective teacher efficacy.

Conditions	Awareness	Emotions	Enhanced
↑	↑	↑	↑
Source of Influence ↔	Paradox ↔	Belief Constructs ↔	Collective Efficacy
↓	↓	↓	↓
Consequences	Actions	Convictions	Diminished

Figure 7.1: Collective teacher efficacy Theory of Action.

The Theory of Action that brings the building of collective teacher efficacy together is based on three distinct understandings.

- Understanding the sources of influence for teams building collective teacher efficacy

- Understanding the paradoxes teams face when building collective teacher efficacy

- Understanding the belief constructs teams have when building collective teacher efficacy

Understanding the sources, paradoxes, and belief constructs can assist schools or districts to further collective awareness, assess current realities of organization, and take necessary actions to enhance collective efficacy.

Another way to consider the interplay between these three factors is by using the Pyramid of Collective Efficacy (see figure 7.2, page 132), which provides a visual representation of the Theory of Action. The three sides of the pyramid—sources of influence, paradoxes, and belief constructs—all work together to help teams and leaders build clarity and understanding of what and how to enhance for collective teacher efficacy. Once leaders have understanding, they can be more strategic about how they address challenges and barriers.

By first identifying the sources, paradoxes, and belief constructs, organizations can begin to see the complexities of their challenges simplified into distinct categories. With evaluation and analysis of each category, organizations can assess their current state and develop potential next steps. The following subsections provide a description of each of the components of the TOA and Pyramid of Collective Efficacy.

Understanding the Source of Influence

The source of influence is the specific area the organization is trying to improve (for example, culture, collaboration, or autonomy). It includes two dimensions: (1) conditions, and (2) consequences. These two dimensions directly impact the level of

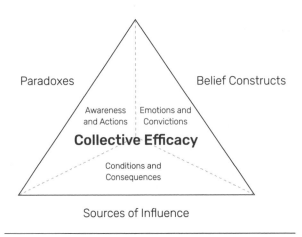

Figure 7.2: The Pyramid of Collective Efficacy.

collective efficacy for teams. A deeper understanding of the source of influence and its dimensions can help bridge awareness and productivity for school organizations.

A team or leader must reflect on a specific question to form a greater understanding of how they might improve collective teacher efficacy. The question is framed as a possible source that might influence positive change that will enhance team efficacy, as follows:

Question: What is the source of influence that will improve team efficacy?

In some cases, the answer to that question for leaders or teams might be "trust," and for others it might be "collaboration." Whatever the source of influence, the team or leader must have a clear understanding that if we improve X (for example, trust), we will improve Y (collective teacher efficacy).

Conditions

The conditions are the environmental factors, including information, that increase or decrease the perceived likelihood of outcomes (for example, focused collaboration, higher degrees of trust, increased buy-in from leadership, and engagement).

As a district, Sanger discovered numerous sources of influence that we needed to improve to build team efficacy. Improving culture had the greatest potential for positive impact on collective teacher efficacy. The conditions that we needed to create were greater trust and collaboration between teachers and administrators. Trust and collaboration could only occur if the organization's leaders were more transparent and honest about both how and what they communicated to the organization. The leaders became keenly aware that they had to create conditions that fostered trusting professional relationships by communicating openly and honestly with their teams.

Consequences

Consequences are the results or outcomes of conditions that reinforce positive or negative perceptions (for example, resiliency attributes, higher expectations, and increased commitment).

The consequences of Sanger's leadership communicating openly and honestly with teams had two outcomes: (1) accessibility of information for teams, and (2) sharing of ideas. Creating access to information helped with clarity for some teams and not for others. In addition, the organization had to consider the consequences of sharing too much information, information that only made the system foggier and more complicated to understand. The organization also had to consider the consequences of sharing too little information, potentially creating even more distrust in the organization because teams could perceive it as a half-hearted effort. The answer came to the organizational leaders when they identified both how and what to communicate. Once the *what* was clear, the potential consequences (positive or negative) led to understanding the *how*, and both of those led to a paradox.

Understanding the Paradox

The paradox involves the perceived, oftentimes opposing actions, behaviors, or views that are required to achieve balance within an initiative or objective (for example, systems vs. people, consistency vs. change, confrontation vs. support, and growth mindset vs. fixed mindset).

Once the source of influence and its conditions and consequences were clearly identified and understood, Sanger's leaders were faced with exploring the paradox or paradoxes within it. The paradox includes two dimensions: (1) awareness, and (2) actions. The paradox helps identify the nuances of opposing constructs, behaviors, or views that are necessary if leadership is to achieve change within the source of influence. Leaders at Sanger wanted to change culture and create conditions of shared and transparent communication and information. The consequences were based on positive and negative mindsets of teams formed by past experiences.

For us, the natural next steps to increase trust and collaboration included establishing new structures, strategy, or operations for the district; creating a new task force for building teacher efficacy (one that gave feedback to the organization); and establishing new policies and guidelines, including jointly created operational manuals for leaders that integrated teacher voice and choice into collective commitments. These next steps may have helped our PLC confront pockets of system dysfunction and build confidence in the organization's ability to persevere. The paradox of improving the system as systems versus people was exposed.

Our understanding of Wheatley's (1992) research led to a unique perspective of trying to avoid system tweaks first. Sanger focused on improving people's ability to trust and collaborate by developing the capacity of leadership through relationship building that would lead to greater trust, interdependence, and collaboration. As those improved, system structures that likewise needed to progress became clearer and less complicated. That is why Sanger continues to thrive—the script was flipped as a result of the mental model. Where most districts would have adopted PLC system change first, Sanger's approach was different. Leaders specifically and strategically focused on relationships and communication that enhanced trust and collaboration, followed by the adoption of the PLC process's form and function.

The following sections will explain the two constructs within the paradox: awareness and actions.

Awareness

Awareness is the identification, acknowledgment, or appreciation of the existence of paradox(es), and the understanding that balance is required (for example, teams recognize the need to move from beyond compliance to self-regulation, or teams recognize the need to balance autonomy within boundaries).

Awareness of the paradox is based on the conditions that might be both positive and negative. For example, leaders must be keenly aware of growth mindsets (those who believed the act of transparent, honest communication and information was malleable) versus fixed mindsets (those whose convictions were set and saw the effort to create transparency as a deception and non-changing) in order to build efficacy. The action to create the right conditions has consequences, both positive and negative. Being aware of the paradox can create clear actions that help the team navigate the necessary experience that needs to be created for change.

We became keenly aware that not all leaders were successful at building trusting relationships and collaboration. Having inspirational visions and the ability to connect with people became increasingly more important characteristics for Sanger's leadership than management styles that had dominated in the past. The ability to engage stakeholders was a characteristic of a successful leader. Awareness of this issue challenged the organization to make decisions about how to support those leaders that struggled to build trust and collaboration or what to do with those leaders who could not build trust and collaboration.

Actions

Actions refer to steps taken as a result of awareness of the paradoxes identified in relation to current reality (for example, increased investment in programs to enhance processes and procedures—systems—versus increased investment in PLC development with an emphasis on values, trust, and collaborative efforts—people).

The organization must then consider what actions to take as a result of being aware of both positive and negative outcomes. Being aware helps a leader or team determine not only what to communicate but also how they might communicate. In our case, it was clear—to enhance culture and ultimately improve collective teacher efficacy, the organization was going to communicate a clear vision about what it wanted to become. Sanger addressed the *how* of this work by stepping away from old processes and old philosophies and letting the new organization work to create visions of its own that were more meaningful to all stakeholders.

The organization had to take actions to re-address its purpose, establish character, and create an identity that gave each member a greater *why* and purpose for his or her work. "Every Child, Every Day, Whatever it Takes" became a motto that was on every paper and every wall and said at every meeting to communicate clearly to the organization that this is who we are and why we do what we do.

Understanding Belief Constructs

Belief constructs are an individual's presumptions or confidence that an outcome (positive or negative) will result due to perceived capabilities (for example, a team possesses negative beliefs regarding school culture within an underlying issue of lack of trust).

Belief constructs include two dimensions: (1) emotions and (2) convictions. Beliefs are typically created as a result of past experiences. The beliefs professionals hold may be associated with strong negative emotions if past experiences led to professional distrust or personal stress. On the other hand, the beliefs professionals hold may be associated with positive emotions if past experiences carried a strong sense of success, fulfillment, and joy. Beliefs may reveal the level of conviction of teams and can help the leader or team anticipate the degree of resistance or openness to change.

For Sanger, negative experiences had fostered a negative belief in leadership and organizational management. Constant changes to organizational goals and site direction and mixed messages, coupled with a "hunker down and leave me alone" attitude, had created negative beliefs in leaders, organizational capacity, and purpose. This negative emotion created strong convictions about how and what needed to get done. Teachers took action into their own hands—the sign "Home of 400 Unhappy Teachers" was raised, and it remains a perfect example of the negative convictions the organization possessed. Any attempt to change beliefs and address convictions was going to be met with resistance, doubt, and negative perceptions.

Emotions

Understanding emotions helps anticipate the associated response to change efforts. Teams with elevated emotions require different, more targeted types of team experiences to offset the intensity. The use of metaphors—visuals of hope for the future—became a key strategy for communicating a greater purpose. Those individuals or teams less prone to displaying their emotions publicly may require additional information and clarity of purpose.

Sanger's leaders understood that even though sharing of information was essential to build trust and collaboration, it alone was not enough. Teams with elevated emotions in relation to the source of influence (culture) would require immediate follow-up from leaders, and more direct opportunities for questions and answers. And in some cases, teams would require a different messenger if they were going to shift away from negative emotional triggers.

Convictions

Convictions refer to the level or degree of certainty within a belief. A high degree of conviction means not easily influenced; a low degree means easily influenced. For example: the third-grade team has zero faith that leadership will ever follow through with what is promised (a high degree of conviction). The ELA department believes that the PLC process is important but has requested additional research and proof that it actually works in order to justify change (low level of conviction).

Understanding the level of conviction or level of certainty or uncertainty of changing minds creates an opportunity for improving team efficacy. In our case, the convictions for some teams, particularly at the high school, were strong. There existed an inability and an unwillingness to trust the leaders and the new system regardless of efforts. In other words, there was little that could be done from their perspective that would change their minds about leadership and attempts to improve culture—unless, however, the leaders were strategic, worked with team influencers, and gave them greater authority, autonomy, and choice on what to change and how they might change. Team members' individual convictions tell leaders the type of experience to create to improve the convictions of teams.

Understanding Potential Outcomes

The purpose of this section is to highlight the experiences teams have as they work to enhance collective teacher efficacy or understand why it has been diminished. It will also describe the lessons Sanger's leadership learned as a result of their experiences.

As leaders and teams become aware of the TOA, they can then move strategically and build collective efficacy. Building collective efficacy of teams requires that leaders be attuned to how their actions may enhance or diminish collective efficacy. Collective efficacy is delicate, and what were positive intentions can easily create negative ripples, and vice versa. What may have been seen as a positive intention can, in some cases, create negative ripples for collective efficacy. To measure improvement, teams and leaders must check for how teams are responding to the changes associated with the source of influence.

Enhanced Collective Efficacy

As the district identified the source of influence (namely, the culture), leaders could then assess the conditions and consequences. The conditions or environment had created a lack of transparency and trust. This resulted in a negative consequence of low expectations for change. Past confidence in the system to be transparent and trustworthy only highlighted an array of emotions and convictions teams held. Understanding the issues helped the leaders identify a set of desired conditions and potential consequences of efforts to improve collective efficacy.

What we realized was that improving culture was key to creating new opportunities for team collaboration and trust building. There was a realization that adding a new initiative, PLCs, to the goals of the district was not the best first step if leadership was to address negative emotions and convictions about the history of organizational change initiatives. Leaders came to realize that any positive intentions of PLCs, no matter how valuable, would be seen as "here we go again," and resistance would be part of every team's mental makeup regardless of the benefits.

Once the leaders understood this potential negative ripple, they were able to take action by building the capabilities of leadership to develop new professional relationships. This built trust and collaboration. Only after seeing negative emotions begin to disappear and convictions begin to change did they insert a new initiative for the work, PLCs.

Diminished Collective Efficacy

The awareness of negative conditions and potential negative consequences associated with collective efficacy leads to clarity for leaders and teams about the existing paradox. The actions the organization chooses to pursue could create improved understanding and acceptance from teams, or potentially lead to greater resistance.

At Sanger, the paradox was creating access to information to enhance trust versus increasing information that may lead to confusion. Stakeholders had applied belief constructs to the change efforts that created the paradox for leaders. Stakeholder beliefs were deeply rooted in the idea that too much information from leaders could lead to stakeholders feeling like there was less understanding, or a deliberate intent to fog and confuse stakeholders. But, if the leaders shared too little information, stakeholders might think it was a halfhearted effort to build rapport and trust.

To build collective efficacy, leaders had to focus on specific, targeted efforts to address each team's beliefs. By being clear and strategic, leaders were able to apply learning that led to successful collective team efficacy, not necessarily acquired at the same time but strategic enough to bring the majority of teams to a place where they trusted the information and believed in the efforts. As a result, teams were able to let go of negative mindsets and replaced them with growth mindsets that led to improved culture and greater collective teacher efficacy.

The Four Types of Experiences That Impact Collective Efficacy

Understanding the Theory of Action allows leaders to shape experiences for teams that can help teams break through barriers that prevent collective team efficacy from forming. Adapted from Bandura's (1986) *Social Foundations of Thought and Action*, the experiences leaders can use to help teams break these barriers are as follows.

- Mastery Experiences

- Vicarious Experiences

- Social Persuasion Experiences

- Affective State Experiences

Table 7.1 lists the characteristics of each type of experience.

TABLE 7.1: EFFICACY-SHAPING EXPERIENCES

Type of Experiences	Definition
Mastery Experiences	Teams experience success and attribute success to causes within their control, and collective efficacy increases. Success breeds belief; failure undermines a sense of collective efficacy.
Vicarious Experiences	Teams see others succeed with the same opportunities and challenges, and they assume that they too can be successful.
Social Persuasion Experiences	Teams are encouraged by credible and trustworthy persuaders to innovate and overcome challenges. Social persuasion "depends on establishing norms of openness, collaboration, and cooperation" (Adams & Forsyth, 2006, p. 631).
Affective State Experiences	Teams experience excitement or anxiety based on their perceptions of their capability or incompetence. According to Goddard, Hoy, and Hoy (2004), "Affective states may influence how organizations interpret and react to the myriad of challenges they face" (p. 6). Tschannen-Moran and Barr (2004) refer to affective states as "the emotional tone of the organization" (p. 190).

Sources: Adams & Forsyth, 2006; Bandura, 1986; Goddard et al., 2004; Tschannen-Moran & Barr, 2004.

Understanding how to create a more positive experience is key to building collective team efficacy. For example, leaders will need to treat a team with strong belief constructs (meaning high emotion and high convictions for change) differently from a team with high emotional resistance toward change and high convictions of resistance to change. To create different experiences, one needs to know how and when to apply specific experiences for the team.

Figures 7.3–7.8 (pages 139–141) show the Collective Efficacy: Degree Quadrant Tool leaders can use to measure the sources of influence, paradoxes, and beliefs their teams are encountering, and the associated type of experience needed to move the team. The use of these quadrants allows leaders and teams to better identify the current state of teams and what experience to create to build collective teacher efficacy. The following quadrants illustrate an example team struggling with the source of influence construct of *collaboration*.

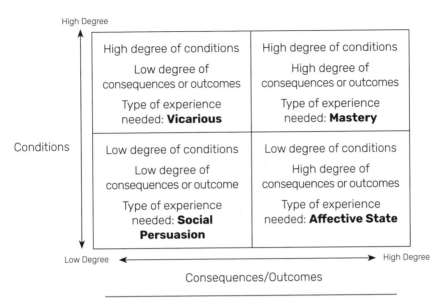

Figure 7.3: Source of influence—collaboration.

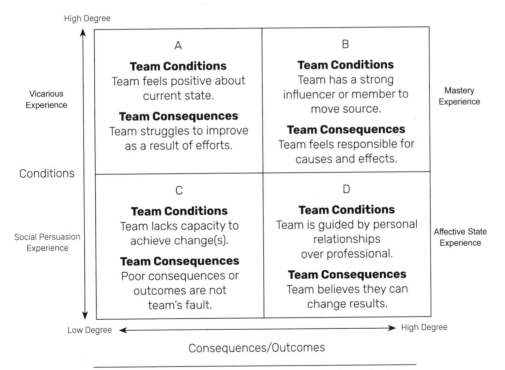

Figure 7.4: Source of influence—team descriptions.

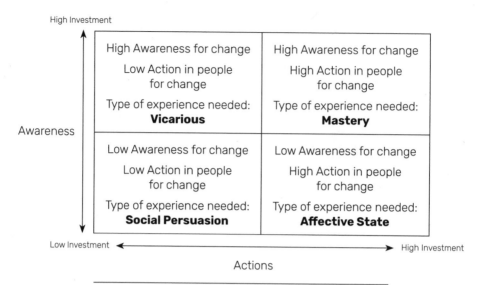

Figure 7.5: Paradoxes—awareness and actions.

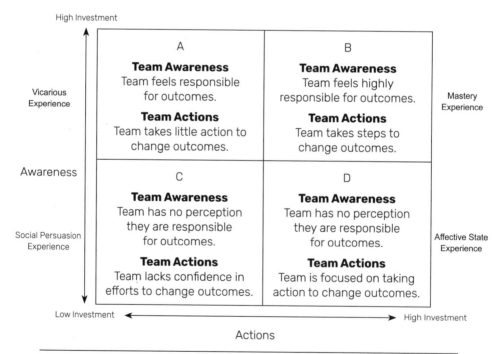

Figure 7.6: Paradoxes—awareness and actions (team descriptions).

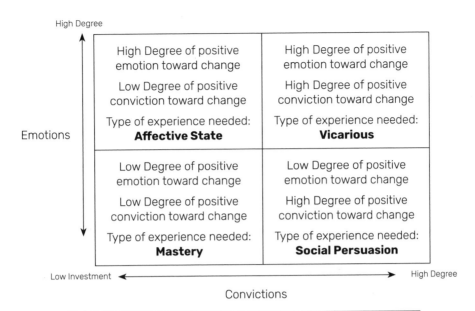

Figure 7.7: Belief constructs—emotions and convictions.

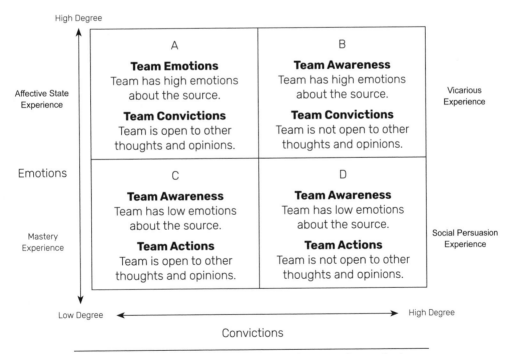

Figure 7.8: Belief constructs—emotions and convictions (team descriptions).

Understanding where teams fall within the quadrant according to the source of influence and what types of experiences a team may need to move toward change is essential in building collective team efficacy. Once the team's current state is identified, the experience for change can be applied, meaning the experience that might be best applied to move the team. The applied experiences are twofold.

1. The more a leader and team can identify where teams are with respect to the source of influence, the more they can construct the right experience.

2. The more a leader or team can construct the right experience, the more likely they are to produce a more strategic approach that will lead to more positive experiences for the team and ultimately build collective team efficacy.

The following examples demonstrate how leaders can use the quadrant tools to effect change in a team by addressing each factor influencing collective efficacy.

Example One: Source of Influence

For example, a leader assesses a third-grade team on the source of influence (collaboration) necessary for the team to build collective team efficacy. The leader understands that there is a gap between collaboration and implementation of collaborative team structures. The third-grade team doesn't have strong resistance to increased collaboration but believes they are already collaborating effectively.

In the "Source of Influence" quadrant, leaders would assess the third-grade team based on positive conditions for collaboration (is the team set up with the basic conditions for positive change?), and potential positive consequences of collaboration (does their current state lead to positive consequences and outcomes?). This third-grade team would sit in the top left quadrant, meaning they have a high degree of positive conditions to make changes, and the current consequences or outcomes are low.

Vicarious experiences would help the identified team see other teams succeed who have the same structure but were producing better outcomes. They might require a visit to another school or team in the district. The reason why this is important is because leaders wouldn't use a vicarious experience on a team with a high degree of conditions for collaboration (meaning they have collaborative team structures in place) and a high degree of consequences. That team wouldn't need convincing or a self-assessment of their impact; rather, that team would need a mastery experience to build more successful working constructs to push the desires of the team. However, the team in the example is not ready for that experience; they believe they are already doing that. So, the experience needed is vicarious; they need to see teams that have their structures but are producing better consequences or outcomes.

Example Two: Paradoxes

The third-grade team displays a paradox in that they have low awareness for change, they are not aware that their structures are ineffective, and they see very little need to take any new action. The team is essentially suffering from the "feeling good vs. doing badly" paradox (see chapter 2, page 41). The third-grade team would need a social persuasion experience.

Teams in the bottom left quadrant would benefit from a credible source or trustworthy persuader. Social persuasion puts a focus on a team influencer first. Working on a single influencer or persuader allows the leader to expand a single member of the team's perception and to have them reconsider the team's abilities. This allows the team to then be persuaded by someone other than leaders or coaches.

Example Three: Belief Constructs

The beliefs of the third-grade team must be assessed to determine the most appropriate type of experience necessary to increase collective efficacy. The team has a low degree of positive emotion for change, meaning they are not motivated by emotions; they believe they are solid in their implementation of collaborative team structures. They also have high convictions; their belief is that they are doing all that has been asked of them. They are making the sacrifices, spending more time sharing, and producing more similar lesson plans. This places the third-grade team in the bottom right quadrant. They have a low degree of emotion for positive change and high convictions for what they are doing. This team doesn't believe it is ineffective, is not swayed by the leader's call to action, and has strong convictions toward and for their efforts.

This three-pronged approach to the assessment of the example third-grade team calls for several experiences—vicarious and social persuasion experiences—that might move the team toward more positive collective team efficacy. This model helps leaders and teams assess their current state and more strategically construct experiences that help build collective team efficacy.

Conclusion: Bringing the Theory of Action All Together

The takeaway from the Theory of Action is that leaders can use it to identify the types of challenges teams have in relationship to collective teacher efficacy and can identify the experiences they need to create for teams to overcome those barriers. "At the heart of system transformation is cultivating collaborative cultures" (Fullan & Quinn, 2016, p. 12). Building collaborative cultures leads to teams working together to overcome the challenges they face. As teams look for ways to work together to overcome their lack of efficacy, the TOA provides an opportunity for teams to assess their current sources of influence and identify the specific issues holding them back from building positive collective teacher efficacy by identifying the following.

- **Source of influence:** Conditions and consequences
- **Paradox:** Awareness and actions of identified source
- **Belief constructs:** Emotions and convictions of identified source

By teams being aware of the sources of influence, paradoxes, and belief constructs they possess, the team, or leader leading the team, can begin to identify the experience (mastery, vicarious, social persuasion, or affective state) that needs to occur to move the team forward.

Next Steps

In this section, we provide the reader some simple next steps to take as a team associated with the learnings from the readings. See the reproducibles "Collective Efficacy: Team Starter Template" (page 145) and "Creating Feedback Cycles and Next Steps for Collective Efficacy" (page 148) for templates to use and a completed example.

- Assess the team's source of influence and the dimensions (conditions and consequences) associated with it.
- Assess the team's paradox and the dimensions (awareness and actions) associated with it.
- Assess the team's belief and the dimensions (emotions and convictions) associated with it.
- Identify one or a combination of the four experiences that need to be created to move the team forward in building collective teacher efficacy.
- Build in ongoing feedback cycles that target next steps for collective efficacy.
- Have the team summarize their results based on ongoing feedback cycles and next steps, then share with other teams to chart continued improvement.

Collective Efficacy: Team Starter Template

General Areas of focus	Team identifies specific *Area(s)* of focus	Specific *Dimension* of identified Area	Team description of current reality in each *Dimension*	Team description of intended reality in each *Dimension*	Team identifies efficacy-shaping *Experiences* and *Actions* necessary to enhance Collective Efficacy
Source of Influence		Conditions			
		Consequences			
Paradox	_____ vs. _____	Awareness			
		Actions			
Belief Construct(s)		Emotions			
		Convictions			

page 1 of 3

Collective Efficacy in a PLC at Work® © 2021 Solution Tree Press

General *Areas* of focus	Team identifies specific *Area*(s) of focus	Specific *Dimension* of identified *Area*	Team description of current reality in each *Dimension*	Team description of intended reality in each *Dimension*	Team identifies efficacy-shaping *Experiences* and *Actions* necessary to enhance **Collective Efficacy**
Source of Influence	i.e., Collaboration	Conditions	Low conditions for structures around team collaboration	Increase to high conditions for collaborative structures.	Vicarious = identify other teams.
		Consequences	Little or no consequences for a lack of collaboration	Increase conditions for consequences associated with a lack of collaboration.	Mastery = Identify a short-term goal for success in two weeks. All teams will hold first collaborative conversation.
Paradox	Collaboration: Structure vs. Autonomy	Awareness	Low awareness among staff for change	Currently staff see little value in collaboration.	Vicarious = Look to other successful teams and find out how they feel about the benefits of collaboration.
		Actions	Little action associated with change	Staff are fearful the structures will compromise their ability to plan.	Mastery = Implement structures for first part of team meetings and allow flexibility for other topics.

page 2 of 3

Collective Efficacy in a PLC at Work® © 2021 Solution Tree Press

Belief Construct(s)		Emotions		Low emotions associated with change	Staff have little emotions tied to collaboration.	Affective state = We need to create positive emotions for change, highlighting what collaboration means for us and what it can do for your students.
	Collaboration is not valued.		Convictions	Low degree of convictions toward change	Staff have low convictions regarding the value for collaboration.	Vicarious = We need to see a school that is experiencing better outcomes and overcoming challenges.

page 3 of 3

Creating Feedback Cycles and Next Steps for Collective Efficacy

General *Areas* of focus	Specific *Dimension* of identified *Area*	Use the Collective Efficacy: Degree Quadrant Tool to build in ongoing feedback cycles and next steps.	Teams summarize results based on ongoing feedback cycles and next steps, then share with all teams to chart continued improvement.
Source of Influence: _____	Conditions		
	Consequences		
Paradox: _____ vs. _____	Awareness		
	Actions		
Belief Construct(s): _____	Emotions		
	Convictions		

Collective Efficacy in a PLC at Work® © 2021 Solution Tree Press

SolutionTree.com • Visit **go.SolutionTree.com/PLCbooks** to download this free reproducible.

EPILOGUE

The final truth to building collective efficacy is threefold: (1) leaders must repeatedly revisit the core definition of collective efficacy and infuse its elements into all facets of the organization; (2) leaders must be willing and able to move teams from practice to theory, and then back to practice, in a cycle that is both frequent and deliberate; and (3) leaders must be fully equipped with a balanced arsenal of skill sets that can be called upon in any given situation or circumstance.

The Core Definition of Collective Efficacy

Leaders must revisit and embed the widely accepted definition of Bandura's (1997) collective efficacy—"a group's shared belief in its conjoint capability to organize and execute the courses of action required to produce given levels of attainment" (p. 477)—into the fabric of the school organization. And it cannot be emphasized enough, as mentioned in chapter 7 (page 129), that John Hattie (2016) ranked collective teacher efficacy as *the greatest factor* impacting student achievement.

The conclusions leaders drew from Sanger's district transformation are crystal clear—the research and information they discovered create the moral imperative for school leaders to find implicit and explicit ways to consistently infuse, shape, and mold the definition of collective efficacy and its parts into the organization's practices and culture. In the end, at the core of collective efficacy, regardless of the nuances within researchers' definitions, is this: a team's belief and confidence in one another to do what is necessary to achieve success are the key ingredients to building collective team efficacy.

Therefore, leaders must ensure that specific, high-leverage actions are personalized for teams and are executed with precision so that the efforts can lead to small team wins. These small team wins (however defined by the organization) will reinforce and enhance collective efficacy over time.

The Practice-Theory-Practice Cycle (PTPC)

It is important to note that the TOA laid out in chapter 7 (page 129) is the direct result of the collective *learning by doing* of the organization. Starting with philosophy, then jumping into practice—not blindly, but with enough information and interdependence for teams to maneuver and refine practices—were the beginning of building collective teacher efficacy. This was followed by the intentionality of building enough professional capacity and coherence to make sound decisions, which directly led to substantial and sustainable increases in student outcomes. Additionally, it is important to note that the ability of the organization to establish a core set of principles, anchored in mission, vision, values, and goals, gave leaders the ability to adapt and the fluidity to adjust their actions in real time for the betterment of student achievement and alignment with the organization's core purpose.

Essentially, Sanger's commitment to collectively *learning by doing* meant they established and adopted an operating theoretical framework that was internalized, owned, and revisited by site leaders frequently. This framework gave practitioners the power and permission to fully execute the details of their responsibilities with meaningful purpose—a purpose fully aligned to the district vision. With ongoing reflection and input, the organization revisited the operating theory to seek opportunities to improve its efficiency and viability. This *Practice-Theory-Practice Cycle* (PTPC) was repeated within and across schools under the guides of a collective district vision and philosophy. Considering this effort and effect on collective efficacy, it is essential for school leaders to recognize not only the importance but the enormous effort that the PTPC may have on transforming culture and generating positive outcomes for students.

A Balanced Arsenal of Leadership Skill Sets

School leaders must understand a critical and important nuance to balanced leadership: it's never balanced. The truth is that balance may be a leadership approach, but it is not essential to organizational success. Furthermore, equilibrium—or as some may envision it, a "euphoria"—in school organizations is truly a myth and cannot be achieved. The broad spectrum of working dynamics of the teachers, leaders, and students within and across the system creates ongoing, never static, moving targets and changes (good or bad) that influence the organization and prevent equilibrium from happening.

The real work that generates the most change exists in the grit, grind, and daily actions of practitioners. Strategic plans and initiatives only make up a small but meaningful part of the entire system that impacts student outcomes. The reality is that the people, not the programs within it, will continue to be the primary catalyst that impacts the space where theory and practice merge. We believe that this collision of theory and practice is the nucleus of change for schools that leads to enhanced collective efficacy. More specifically, we believe that leaders who are appropriately equipped with the capability and confidence to influence this space are profoundly more likely to inspire powerful school cultures and produce transformational outcomes for teams.

Therefore, the key to building collective efficacy in teams is to fully equip leaders with a balanced arsenal of capacity, coherence, and skills necessary to make timely and sound decisions that lead to positive change. This formula will help leaders bring to life the vision of building collective efficacy across the organization. Being equipped with this balanced arsenal will allow leaders to accurately and authentically assess individuals and teams, then directly apply a prescription to produce better results. Regardless, leaders must be equipped with the leadership skills that allow them to seamlessly navigate the complex web of systems to specifically address the needs and demands of teams.

Conclusion

The culmination of this book reinforces the research and practices that claim building collective team efficacy is critical to ongoing improvement in all facets of the organization. School leadership must be simultaneously fierce yet delicate. Building collective efficacy isn't about probability or effective versus ineffective practices; rather, it is about belief, conviction, and the willingness to do "whatever it takes" for students! And don't forget, collective efficacy is about commitment to a better vision—a vision that believes it can change a sign from the "Home of 400 Unhappy Teachers" to a sign that says, "Welcome to Sanger: Home of 400 Happy Teachers!"

APPENDIX

The appendix contains the following reproducibles for general use:

1-5-10 Analysis Tool (Individual)

Statement Scores	Actions or Practices
What statements are identified as 1, 5, and 10? (Sort by statement scoring.) 1s: 5s: 10s:	Actions or practices necessary to attain or maintain 10 status:
What do you notice, based on the statement scores, simply at a glance?	Actions or practices necessary to improve 5 to 10 status:
What areas, based on statement scores, may potentially require additional processing time?	Actions or practices necessary to improve 1 to 5 status:
What might be considered three areas of strength?	What might be considered three areas of growth?

Collective Efficacy in a PLC at Work® © 2021 Solution Tree Press

SolutionTree.com • Visit **go.SolutionTree.com/PLCbooks** to download this free reproducible.

1–5–10 Analysis Tool (Team)

Questions to Consider for Teams' Statement Scores	Notes
What do you notice or wonder about the 1–5–10 summary scores for teams?	
What do you notice or wonder about the similarities or differences between 1–5–10 statement scores across categories?	
What areas, based on summary score averages, may potentially require further team discussion?	
What might be considered three areas of strength for the team?	
What might be considered three areas of growth for the team?	

Collective Efficacy in a PLC at Work® © 2021 Solution Tree Press

SolutionTree.com • Visit **go.SolutionTree.com/PLCbooks** to download this free reproducible.

1–5–10 Team Summary Tool: Category Comparison Example

Teacher Names	Category: Vision	Category: Culture	Category: Autonomy
Teacher A	75	80	26
Teacher B	80	75	53
Teacher C	61	70	26
Teacher D	71	47	51
Teacher E	75	76	68
Teacher F	70	71	60
Teacher G	65	66	47
Teacher H	70	61	26
Teacher I	80	75	43
Teacher J	80	58	31
Teacher K	80	62	31
Teacher L	95	85	76
Teacher M	68	27	30
Teacher N	62	56	42
Teacher O	62	70	53
Teacher P	70	57	34
Teacher Q	65	47	34
Teacher R	66	51	35
Teacher S	75	54	35
Teacher T	66	58	18
Teacher U	71	48	51
Teacher V	66	58	18
Teacher W	57	63	39
	1,630 Total Points /23 Teachers	1,415 Total Points /23 Teachers	927 Total Points /23 Teachers

1–5–10 Summary Tool (Tri-Annual): Beginning, Middle, and End-of-Year Comparison Example for One Category (Example Category—Measurement)

Teacher Name	Beginning of Year	Middle of Year	End of Year
Teacher A	50	64	73
Teacher B	62	62	67
Teacher C	81	95	95
Teacher D	80	91	95
Teacher E	46	50	56
Teacher F	55	63	55
Teacher G	46	62	73
Teacher H	67	80	91
Teacher I	51	60	70
Teacher J	90	95	95

REFERENCES AND RESOURCES

Adams, C. M., & Forsyth, P. B. (2006). Proximate sources of collective teacher efficacy. *Journal of Educational Administration, 44*(6), 626–642.

Bailey, K., & Jakicic, C. (2012). *Common formative assessment: A toolkit for Professional Learning Communities at Work*. Bloomington, IN: Solution Tree Press.

Bandura, A. (1977). Self-efficacy: Toward a unifying theory of behavioral change. *Psychological Review*, 84(2), 191–215.

Bandura, A. (1986). *Social foundations of thought and action: A social cognitive theory*. Englewood Cliffs, NJ: PrenticeHall.

Bandura, A. (1997). *Self-efficacy: The exercise of control*. New York: Freeman.

Bloomberg, P., & Pitchford, B. (2017). *Leading impact teams: Building a culture of efficacy*. Thousand Oaks, CA: Corwin Press.

Bryant, A. (2014, January 4). Management be nimble. *The New York Times*. Accessed at www.nytimes.com/2014/01/05/business/management-be-nimble.html?_r=0 on September 10, 2015.

California Department of Education. (n.d.). *Jefferson Elementary School API, 1998–2010*. Accessed at www.cde.ca.gov on November 15, 2019.

California Statewide Task Force on Special Education. (2015). *2015 Report of California's Statewide Task Force*. Accessed at www.cde.ca.gov/sp/se/sr/taskforce2015.asp on December 22, 2020.

Caproni, P. J. (2017). *The science of success: What researchers know that you should know*. Ann Arbor, MI: Van Rye.

Collaborate. (n.d.). In *Merriam-Webster.com*. Accessed at www.merriam-webster.com/dictionary/collaborate on April 21, 2021.

Collins, J. (2009). *How the mighty fall: And why some companies never give in*. New York: HarperCollins.

Collins, J., & Porras, J. (1996). Building your company's vision. Harvard Business Review, 74(5), 65–77.

Connors, R., & Smith, T. (2011). *Change the culture, change the game: The breakthrough strategy for energizing your organization and creating accountability for results.* New York: Portfolio.

Couros, G. (2015). *The innovator's mindset: Empower learning, unleash talent, and lead a culture of creativity.* San Diego, CA: Burgess.

Covey, S. R. (2004). *The eighth habit: From effectiveness to greatness.* New York: Free Press.

Covey, S. R. (2015). *Primary greatness: The 12 levers of success.* New York: Simon & Schuster.

Covey, S. M. R., & Merrill, R. R. (2006). *The speed of trust: The one thing that changes everything.* New York: Free Press.

David, J. L., & Talbert, J. E. (2013). *Turning around a high poverty district: Learning from Sanger.* San Francisco: S. H. Cowell Foundation.

Deal, T. E., & Peterson, K. D. (2002). *Shaping school culture: Pitfalls, paradoxes, and promises* (1st ed.). San Francisco: Jossey-Bass.

Deal, T. E., & Peterson, K. D. (2009). *Shaping school culture: Pitfalls, paradoxes, and promises* (2nd ed.). San Francisco: Jossey-Bass.

DeWitt, P. M. (2018). *School climate: Leading with collective efficacy.* Thousand Oaks, CA: Corwin Press.

Dixon, C. (2019). *A framework for executive leadership of continuous improvement in K-12 public school districts: Learning from research and practice.* Doctoral dissertation, University of Virginia, Charlottesville. Accessed at https://libraetd.lib.virginia.edu/public_view /g445cd68w on May 17, 2021.

Donohoo, J. (2017). *Collective efficacy: How educators' beliefs impact student learning.* Thousand Oaks, CA: Corwin Press.

Donohoo, J., Hattie, J., & Eells, R. (2018). The power of collective efficacy. *Educational Leadership, 75*(6), 40–44.

Donohoo, J., & Katz, S. (2020). *Quality implementation: Leveraging collective efficacy to make "what works" actually work.* Thousand Oaks, CA: Corwin Press.

Donohoo, J., & Velasco, M. (2016). *The transformative power of collaborative inquiry: Realizing change in schools and classrooms.* Thousand Oaks, CA: Corwin Press.

Drucker, P. (1992). *Managing for the future: The 1990s and beyond.* New York: Truman Talley Books/Dutton.

Duckworth, A. (2016). *Grit: The power of passion and perseverance.* New York: Scribner.

DuFour, R. (2016, Summer). *Loose vs. tight. AllThingsPLC Magazine,* 33.

DuFour, R., & DuFour, R. (2012). *The school leader's guide to Professional Learning Communities at Work.* Bloomington, IN: Solution Tree Press.

DuFour, R., DuFour, R., Eaker, R., & Many, T. (2006). *Learning by doing: A handbook for Professional Learning Communities at Work.* Bloomington, IN: Solution Tree Press.

DuFour, R., DuFour, R., Eaker, R., & Many, T. (2010). *Learning by doing: A handbook for Professional Learning Communities at Work* (2nd ed.). Bloomington, IN: Solution Tree Press.

DuFour, R., DuFour, R., Eaker, R., Many, T. W., & Mattos, M. (2016). *Learning by doing: A handbook for professional learning communities at work* (3rd ed.). Bloomington, IN: Solution Tree Press.

DuFour, R., & Fullan, M. (2013). *Cultures built to last: Systemic PLCs at work.* Bloomington, IN: Solution Tree Press.

DuFour, R., & Marzano, R. J. (2011). *Leaders of learning: How district, school, and classroom leaders improve student achievement.* Bloomington, IN: Solution Tree Press.

Duhigg, C. (2016). *Smarter, faster, better: The secrets of being productive in life and business.* New York: Random House.

Eaker, R., & Keating, J. (2012). *Every school, every team, every classroom: District leadership for growing Professional Learning Communities at Work.* Bloomington, IN: Solution Tree Press.

The Education Trust—West. (2011). *Ed Trust—West grades and ranks California's large, unified school districts to reveal how well they are serving their African-American, Latino and low-income students.* Accessed at https://west.edtrust.org/press-release/ed-trustwest-grades -and-ranks-californias-large-unified-school-districts-to-reveal-how-well-they-are-serving -their-african-american-latino-and-low-income-students-3/ on November 16, 2020.

Eells, R. J. (2011). *Meta-analysis of the relationship between collective teacher efficacy and student achievement.* Unpublished doctoral dissertation, Loyola University Chicago.

Elmore, R. (2004). *School reform from the inside out: Policy, practice, and performance.* Cambridge, MA: Harvard Education Press.

Forsyth, P. B., Adams, C. M., & Hoy, W. K. (2011). *Collective trust: Why schools can't improve without it.* New York: Teachers College Press.

Frankl, V. E. (2006). *Man's search for meaning* (I. Lasch, Trans). Boston: Beacon Press. (Original work published 1946)

Fullan, M. (2010). *Motion leadership: The skinny on becoming change savvy.* Thousand Oaks, CA: Corwin Press.

Fullan, M. (2013). *Motion leadership in action: More skinny on becoming change savvy.* Thousand Oaks, CA: Corwin Press.

Fullan, M. (2019). *Nuance: Why some leaders succeed and others fail.* Thousand Oaks, CA: Corwin Press.

Fullan, M., & Quinn, J. (2016). *Coherence: The right drivers in action for schools, districts, and systems.* Thousand Oaks, CA: Corwin Press.

Fullan, M., Quinn, J., & McEachen, J. (2018). *Deep learning: Engage the world, change the world.* Thousand Oaks, CA: Corwin Press.

Gallo, C. (2011). *The innovation secrets of Steve Jobs: Insanely different principles for breakthrough success.* New York: McGraw-Hill.

George, B. (2015). *True north: Discover your authentic leadership.* San Francisco: Jossey-Bass.

Goddard, R. D., Hoy, W. K., & Hoy, A. W. (2000). Collective teacher efficacy: Its meaning, measure, and impact on student achievement. *American Educational Research Journal, 37*(2), 479–507.

Goddard, R. D., Hoy, W. K., & Hoy, A. W. (2004). Collective efficacy beliefs: Theoretical developments, empirical evidence, and future directions. *Educational Researcher*, *33*(3), 3–13.

Goleman, D. (2013). *Focus: The hidden driver of excellence.* New York: Harper.

Graham, P., & Ferriter, B. (2008). One step at a time. *Journal of Staff Development*, *29*(3), 38–42.

Gray, J. (2016). Investigating the role of collective trust, collective efficacy, and enabling school structures on overall school effectiveness. *Education Leadership Review*, *17*(1), 114–128.

Guerra, P. L., & Wubbena, Z. C. (2017). Teacher beliefs and classroom practices: Cognitive dissonance in high stakes test-influenced environments. *Issues in Teacher Education*, *26*(1). Accessed at https://files.eric.ed.gov/ fulltext/EJ1139327.pdf on June 1, 2021.

Hall, P., & Simeral, A. (2008). *Building teachers' capacity for success: A collaborative approach for coaches and school leaders.* Alexandria, VA: Association for Supervision and Curriculum Development.

Hannigan, J. D., & Hannigan, J. E. (2020). *Building behavior: The educator's guide to evidence-based initiatives.* Thousand Oaks, CA: Corwin Press.

Hattie, J. (2009). *Visible learning: A synthesis of over 800 meta-analyses relating to achievement.* New York: Routledge.

Hattie, J. (2012). *Visible learning for teachers: Maximizing impact on learning.* New York: Routledge.

Hattie, J. (2016, July). *Mindframes and maximizers* [Conference presentation]. Presented at the third annual Visible Learning Conference, Washington, D.C.

Hattie, J. (2017). *250+ influences on student achievement.* Accessed at https://visible-learning .org/wp-content/uploads/2018/03/VLPLUS-252-Influences-Hattie-ranking-DEC-2017.pdf on August 7, 2020.

Hattie, J. (2018). *Collective teacher efficacy (CTE) according to John Hattie.* Accessed at https:// visible-learning.org/2018/03/collective-teacher-efficacy-hattie/ on August 7, 2020.

Hattie, J., & Zierer, K. (2018). *10 mindframes for visible learning: Teaching for success.* New York: Routledge.

Henley, D., & Lynch, S. (1994). Learn to be still [Recorded by the Eagles]. On *Hell freezes over.* Santa Monica, CA: Geffen.

Hoy, W. K., & Sweetland, S. R. (2000). School bureaucracies that work: Enabling, not coercive. *Journal of School Leadership*, *10*(6), 525–541.

Hoy, W. K., & Sweetland, S. R. (2007). Designing better schools: The meaning and nature of enabling school structure. In W. K. Hoy & M. DiPaola (Eds.), *Essential ideas for the reform of American schools* (pp. 339–366). Charlotte, NC: Information Age.

Hoy, W. K., & Tschannen-Moran, M. (2003). The conceptualization and measurement of faculty trust in schools: The omnibus T-scale. In W. K. Hoy & C. Miskel (Eds.), *Studies in leading and organizing schools* (pp. 181–208). Charlotte, NC: Information Age.

HumanMemory.net. (2020). *Neocortex*. Accessed at https://human-memory.net/neocortex/ on December 20, 2020.

Institute for Healthcare Improvement. (n.d.). *Force field analysis* [Video file]. Accessed at www.ihi.org/education/IHIOpenSchool/resources/Pages/AudioandVideo/Whiteboard19 .aspx on October 2, 2020.

Johnson, M. (2015). *How to coach leadership in a PLC*. Bloomington, IN: Solution Tree Press.

Kanold, T. D. (2011). *The five disciplines of PLC leaders*. Bloomington, IN: Solution Tree Press.

Kanold, T. D. (2017). *HEART! Fully forming your professional life as a teacher and leader*. Bloomington, IN: Solution Tree Press.

Kanold, T. D., & Larson, M. R. (2015). *Beyond the Common Core: A handbook for mathematics in a PLC at Work, leader's guide* (T. D. Kanold, Ed.). Bloomington, IN: Solution Tree Press.

Kanold, T., Schuhl, S., Larson, M. R., Barnes, B., Kanold-McIntyre, J., & Toncheff, M. (2018). *Mathematics assessment and intervention in a PLC at Work*. Bloomington, IN: Solution Tree Press.

Katz, S., Earl, L. M., & Jaafar, S. B. (2009). *Building and connecting learning communities: The power of networks for school improvement*. Thousand Oaks, CA: Corwin Press.

Kluger, J. (2008). *Simplexity: Why simple things become complex (and how complex things can be made simple)*. New York: Hyperion.

Kramer, S. V., & Schuhl, S. (2017). *School improvement for all: A how-to guide for doing the right work*. Bloomington, IN: Solution Tree Press.

Lai, E., & Cheung, D. (2015). Enacting teacher leadership: The role of teachers in bringing about change. *Educational Management Administration & Leadership, 43*(5), 673–692.

Lencioni, P. (2002). *The five dysfunctions of a team: A leadership fable*. San Francisco: Jossey-Bass.

Lencioni, P. (2012). *The advantage: Why organizational health trumps everything else in business*. San Francisco: Jossey-Bass.

Leotti, L. A., & Delgado, M. R. (2011). The inherent reward of choice. *Psychological Science, 22*(10), 1310–1318.

Marcos, T., Wise, D., Padover, W., Belenardo, S., & Loose, W. (2018). *How urban California educators engage academic optimism to maximize equity in student learning within socio-economic status (SES) schools*. Accessed at www.californiaeducationalresearchassociation .org/uploads/5/9/6/3/59634897/0002-how-urban-california-educators-engage-academic -opt.pdf on May 17, 2021.

Martin, K. (2012). *The outstanding organization*. New York: McGraw Hill.

Marzano, R. J. (2017). *The new art and science of teaching*. Bloomington, IN: Solution Tree Press.

Marzano, R. J., & Waters, T. (2009). *District leadership that works: Striking the right balance*. Bloomington, IN: Solution Tree Press.

Maslow, A. H. (1943). A theory of human motivation. *Psychological Review, 50*(4), 370–396.

Maslow, A. H. (1954). *Motivation and personality*. New York: Harper.

Mattos, M., DuFour, R., DuFour, R., Eaker, R., & Many, T. (2016). *Concise answers to frequently asked questions about Professional Learning Communities at Work.* Bloomington, IN: Solution Tree Press.

Maxwell, J. C. (2005). *The 360° leader: Developing your influence from anywhere in the organization.* Nashville, TN: Nelson Business.

Maxwell, J. C. (2014). *Good leaders ask great questions: Your foundation for successful leadership.* New York: Center Street.

McChesney, C., Covey, S., & Huling, J. (2012). *The four disciplines of execution: Achieving your wildly important goals.* New York: Free Press.

McLeod, S. (2018). *Cognitive dissonance.* Accessed at www.simplypsychology.org/cognitive -dissonance.html on January 27, 2020.

Melena, S. (2018). *Supportive accountability: How to inspire people and improve performance.* La Mesa, CA: Melena Consulting Group.

Mitchell, R. M., Sun, J., Zhang, S., Mendiola, B., & Tarter, C. J. (2015). School effectiveness: A meta-analytic review of published research. In M. DiPaola & W. K. Hoy (Eds.), *Leadership and school quality* (pp. 161–170). Charlotte, NC: Information Age.

Muhammad, A., & Cruz, L. F. (2019). *Time for change: Four essential skills for transformational school and district leaders.* Bloomington, IN: Solution Tree Press.

Muhammad, A. (2009). *Transforming school culture: How to overcome staff division.* Bloomington, IN: Solution Tree Press.

Muhammad, A. (2018, June 27). *The will to lead: Working together to create a PLC culture* [Keynote address]. Presented at the Professional Learning Communities at Work Institute, Santa Clara, CA.

Noguera, P. (2018, October 18). *Excellence through equity.* [Keynote address]. Presented at the Exemplary Practices in Educational Leadership Conference, Clovis, CA.

O'Day, J. A., & Smith, M. S. (2019). *Opportunity for all: A framework for quality and equality in education.* Cambridge, MA: Harvard Education Press.

Oxford Lexico. (n.d.). *Clarity.* Accessed at www.lexico.com/definition/clarity on January 20, 2021.

Peters, T. J., & Waterman, R. H., Jr. (1982). *In search of excellence: Lessons from America's best-run companies.* New York: Harper & Row.

Pink, D. H. (2009). *Drive: The surprising truth about what motivates us.* New York: Riverhead Books.

Rath, T., & Conchie, B. (2008). *Strengths based leadership: Great leaders, teams, and why people follow.* New York: Gallup Press.

Reeves, D. (2006). *The learning leader: How to focus school improvement for better results.* Alexandria, VA: Association for Supervision and Curriculum Development.

Sanger District Chamber of Commerce. (n.d.). *Trek to the nation's Christmas tree history.* Accessed at https://sanger.org/nation-christmas-tree-city-history/#:~:text=On%20 October%201%2C%201949%2C%20Sanger,the%20Nation's%20Christmas%20 Tree%20City on October, 3, 2020.

Schmoker, M. (2016). *Leading with focus: Elevating the essentials for school and district improvement.* Alexandria, VA. Association for Supervision and Curriculum Development.

Schuhl, S. (2018, June 25–27). *Focusing teams and students with learning targets* [Conference presentation]. Presented at the PLC at Work Institute, Santa Clara, CA.

ScienceDaily.com. (n.d.). *Neocortex (brain).* Accessed at www.sciencedaily.com/terms /neocortex.htm#:~:text=The%20neocortex%20is%20part%20of,%2C%20and%20in%20 humans%2C%20language on December 20, 2020.

Sinek, S. (2009). *Start with why: How great leaders inspire everyone to take action.* New York: Portfolio.

Sinek, S. (2019). *The infinite game.* New York: Portfolio.

Smith, W. R. (2015). *How to launch PLCs in your district.* Bloomington, IN: Solution Tree Press.

Strategies for Influence. (n.d.) *Bill Gates—Coaching quotes and tips.* Accessed at https:// strategiesforinfluence.com/bill-gates-advice/ on December 20, 2020.

Tschannen-Moran, M., & Barr, M. (2004). Fostering student learning: The relationship of collective teacher efficacy and student achievement. *Leadership and Policy in Schools, 3*(3), 189–209.

Warrick, P. B. (2020). High reliability leadership. In R. Eaker & R. J. Marzano (Eds.), *Professional Learning Communities at Work and high reliability schools* (pp. 307–327). Bloomington, IN: Solution Tree Press.

Wheatley, M. J. (1992). *Leadership and the new science: Discovering order in a chaotic world.* Oakland, CA: Berrett-Koehler.

Williams, K. C., & Hierck, T. (2015). *Starting a movement: Building culture from the inside out in professional learning communities.* Bloomington, IN: Solution Tree Press.

Wiseman, L., Allen, L., & Foster, E. (2013). *The multiplier effect: Tapping the genius inside our schools.* Thousand Oaks, CA: Corwin Press.

Zuieback, S. (2012). *Leadership practices for challenging times: Principles, skills and processes that work.* Washington, DC: DG Creative.

INDEX

Learning by Doing, Third Edition
Richard DuFour, Rebecca DuFour, Robert Eaker,
Thomas W. Many, and Mike Mattos
Discover how to transform your school or district into a high-performing PLC. The third edition of this comprehensive action guide offers new strategies for addressing critical PLC topics, including hiring and retaining new staff, creating team-developed common formative assessments, and more.
BKF746

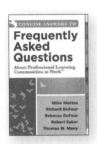

Concise Answers to Frequently Asked Questions About Professional Learning Communities at Work®
Mike Mattos, Richard DuFour, Rebecca DuFour,
Robert Eaker, and Thomas W. Many
Get all of your PLC questions answered. Designed as a companion resource to *Learning by Doing: A Handbook for Professional Learning Communities at Work®* (3rd ed.), this powerful, quick-reference guidebook is a must-have for teachers and administrators working to create and sustain the PLC process.
BKF705

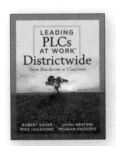

Leading PLCs at Work® Districtwide
Robert Eaker, Mike Hagadone, Janel Keating,
and Meagan Rhoades
Ensure your district is doing the right work, the right way, for the right reasons. With this resource as your guide, you will learn how to align the work of every PLC team districtwide—from the boardroom to the classroom.
BKF942

Leading PLCs at Work® Districtwide Plan Book
Robert Eaker, Mike Hagadone, Janel Keating,
and Meagan Rhoades
Champion continuous improvement with the support of our *Leading PLCs at Work® Districtwide Plan Book*. Divided into weekly and monthly planning pages, the plan book helps guide leaders in identifying and acting upon major responsibilities, tasks, and goals throughout the year.
BKG004

Solution Tree | Press
a division of
Solution Tree

Visit SolutionTree.com or call 800.733.6786 to order.